HIBROW COW

More Alaskan Stories & Recipes
From the Author of Lowbush Moose
Gordon R. Nelson

Alaska Northwest Books™

Anchorage • Seattle

Library of Congress Cataloging-in-Publication Data

Nelson, Gordon R., 1922-
    Hibrow cow / by Gordon R. Nelson ; illustrated by David Berger.
     p.   cm.
    Includes index
    ISBN 0-88240-354-0
    1. Cookery--Alaska.   I. Title.
TX715.N4285   1989   89-15018
641.59798--dc20   CIP

Edited by Ethel Dassow
Book design by Kate Thompson
Illustrations by David Berger

Alaska Northwest Books™
A division of GTE Discovery Publications, Inc.
22026 20th Ave. S.E., Bothell, WA 98021
(206) 487-6100 • 1-800-331-3510

CONTENTS

CHAPTER 1

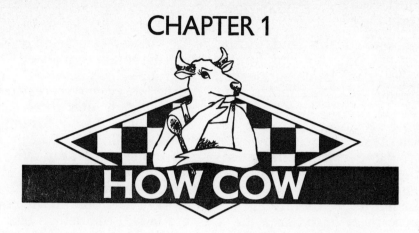

HOW COW

When a writer has three successful books in print, he's always looking for just the right title for his next effort. My three cookbooks, *Lowbush Moose, Smokehouse Bear* and *Tired Wolf* certainly got attention for their titles. The appetite appeal of the recipes sold the books. (I like to think my reminiscing and homespun wisdom helped, too.)

It seems an offbeat title seduces people into looking inside a book, and if they like what they see, they buy it for themselves and maybe for a gift. A gratifying number of those who have my books, by purchase or as gifts, are now my friends. A few have encouraged me to write more books, and have even suggested tantalizing titles.

Consider the confidence displayed by the ones who came up with *Highbrow Cow!* Obviously they thought I could take a new title, gather a few thousand words, and produce a salable book. I was flattered. (All right, I admit it: there were several other ideas about what I should do, some of them not so flattering.) I printed the proposed title on a card and pinned it to the wall behind my computer.

Month after month, as I lifted my eyes for inspiration, I would see "Highbrow Cow" in bold black letters. It wormed its way into my subconscious, wherever that is, and eventually rose as a challenge. All those confident people out there, waiting patiently for my fourth cookbook — how could I disappoint them? I accepted the challenge and this is the book. You'll note that the "Highbrow" has been shortened to "Hibrow." Alaskans are thrifty with everything that's imported.

To me, a lifelong Alaskan and in my younger years a dedicated hunter, "cow" said "cow moose." In this land, during the hunting season, the avid hunter meets females of the game species far more often than he meets males, and usually it's illegal to shoot a cow moose. I have spent countless hours in the field, glasses pressed hard to my eyes, trying to grow antlers on some moose-like creature out there. With a large, hungry family at home, I had to find an antlered animal to get us through the winter. Moose meat found great favor with the growing appetites around our table.

For a while we were stationed in the Matanuska Valley just north of Anchorage, then known for its dairy herds. Inevitably some meat from the common-type cow found its way to our table, but none of that was ever graded "choice" or Hibrow Cow. I bought the old-cow meat. It was cheaper.

Back to the book: I took to asking people on the street or in the stores, "Would a book with the title of *Hibrow Cow* appeal to you?"

Mable M. answered, "It's a goofy title and it might bring my eyes back for a second look."

I rated her answer five on a scale of one to ten.

Tim D. said, "I'd take a look at it. Reminds me of another book, *Lowbush Moose.* Wish I could remember the author's name."

He rated it eight on the second look, but a flat zero for not remembering the author's name.

Gladys F. got the first ten rating. She said, "I'd check the author's name. If it was Gordon R. Nelson, I'd buy three copies. One for my mother in Iowa, one for my sister, and one for me."

My survey completed, I sat down to the computer and added the writing program — the one with the huge spelling dictionary, words created since 1988 not included. After three days of total writer's block I went fishing. Sitting in the boat, drifting on the lake with a line over the side, I let my mind drift back over the last sixty years. Moments of memory came and went like a personal newsreel in an old movie house. Some were faded, the details blurred. Those are the best kind, as the facts don't interfere with creative storytelling.

What was a cow to me? In one of those early memories, aboard one of the ships Dad had skippered, the sailors were discussing "cow palaces." My young mind generated a handsome barn with a clean, neat stall for each cow, and the cows yielded milk for children. Later I learned that a cow palace was where women of the oldest profession plied their trade. Well, that's how my older brother explained it.

Then there was the time Dad was towing a barge loaded with a couple thousand cases of canned salmon, and he commented, "This blank-blank barge steers like a blank-blank cow!" As you can see, I had a varied education. Shortly thereafter I witnessed a violent fight on the afterdeck of the ship. Even a bucket of cold sea water didn't restore the loser's interest in fighting, and Dad remarked, "He's cowed for keeps!" I've never liked to hear the term applied to a loser who has fought well.

Enough about cows. Let's consider "hibrow" or, if you please, "highbrow." I first heard that word as a term of contempt, a contempt often as unreal as the attitude of the person upon whom it was bestowed.

I always liked Mother's definition of a highbrow. "A person who displays characteristics different from your own, usually one who has, or affects, a highly cultivated style of life, or intellectual taste." Now, aren't you glad you bought this book?

Which reminded me of Charles Simms, known as the Lovable Highbrow. There never was a question in anyone's mind; Charles came to Alaska to escape something. A bad marriage? Murder? Embezzlement of company funds? Maybe even a fear that someone was out to kill him?

Charles, as he was known to one and all (never Charlie), was not a lazy man. He worked at the roughest jobs around the waterfront, keeping up with the others, and playing with them as well, but he always showed class. He visited the cow palaces, yes, but he would drink only one expensive brand of whiskey, and he would be served by only the best girl in the house. He never used foul language for any reason.

Strange as it may seem, the other men didn't resent Charles's refined ways. In fact, they were proud of him in a very personal way. His death was a tragedy to the entire community.

The longshoremen were unloading cargo from a ship. The winchman brought a pallet-load out of the hold and it swung toward Charles. Every crewman who saw the danger yelled a warning to Charles. Instead of jumping first and looking later, he turned sedately, with class, to appraise the danger. A corner of the pallet hit him in the chest and

crushed him against the side of the ship. The crew buried him in a new suit, and everyone attended the funeral. I still remember my brother's comment: "Charles was a highbrow in a lowbrow job. Someone yelled 'Duck!' and he turned to see how it was being served."

Back in school that fall, I found that yet another new teacher had come to Alaska to instruct the heathen young locals. Her name was Miss Trillsdale, and I was in her class. She was a small, delicate woman with features carved in stone, and black hair drawn back into a bun. She looked the part of a witch we'd seen pictures of, and she spoke with what Mother called a Boston accent. I anticipated a long, hard year in school.

Mother met Miss Trillsdale at the first PTA meeting, and came home with the knowledge that I had been teasing Beth O'Neal and was now sitting in the front row, under the ruler's touch, so to speak. Mother thought Miss Trillsdale was a very intelligent, well-bred young woman, a true highbrow, and she used the term without contempt.

By Christmas I was in love with Miss Trillsdale. She would stand in front of the class and look directly at me as she talked. The rest of the class were just eavesdroppers so far as I was concerned. No, I didn't want to stay and stare at her during midterm vacation. I wasn't that much in love!

We returned from vacation to find a different Miss Trillsdale with us. This one did not smile. She would jump and turn with panic in her eyes at the slightest noise. Some kids made noises just to see her react. Not me!

In early March we had a substitute teacher, and it was rumored that Miss

Trillsdale was testifying in court. We got no answers to the questions we asked in school, so I took mine home. Mother blushed and sent me to talk to Dad. I worried lest I had done something to offend Mother.

Actually, I had two fathers. One was Dad, the man I saw around home. The other was The Captain, whom I knew well aboard ship. I watched Dad mentally putting on The Captain's hat to answer my question. It was going to be a dead-serious discussion.

He went straight to the point. "Son, during Christmas vacation one of the roomers at the boardinghouse where Miss Trillsdale lives attacked her. He did her bodily harm. He has been arrested and is being tried in court."

"She wasn't bruised when she came back to school," I blurted.

It was Dad who explained, in a softer voice, "She is a small and delicate woman, Son. She suffered great mental and bodily harm that is not evident to others."

"I'm sorry she was hurt," I said, "and I will tell her so when she comes back to school."

"No, Son! This is not the kind of injury a woman wishes to be reminded of. Just be polite and respectful. She will know how you feel. And do not discuss this with anyone." That last was The Captain speaking.

Looking back, I marvel at the ability of the community to keep the event almost secret. I can only assume that the entire community felt a degree of guilt that such a nice young woman had been so badly mistreated while among them.

She was strong and brave enough to finish the school year before she left.

Yes, she was a true highbrow. She had class.

But now it's time to delve into my huge files and present you with some recipes. Do not expect to find far-out recipes, the kind that require you to search for exotic ingredients, and you won't need a dictionary to interpret the instructions. I'm just not that kind of cook. I'm an eater's cook. I love to eat, and to cook.

That did it, now I'm hungry. The writing will have to wait until after dinner. You don't have to wait. Try one of these for a couple of your meals. Enjoy!

HOW COW
JONESVILLE PIE

The number of people in Alaska's Matanuska Valley who remember when it was once a major coal-producing area grows smaller each year. The mines brought the coal miners to the valley and with them came recipes to be passed around. We named this one after one of the old mines. A strange but tasty comment.

1 pound beef, ground round
1 cup chopped onions
1 green pepper, chopped
1 8-ounce can tomato sauce
1 cup corn, canned whole-kernel,
    drained
2 tablespoons mild chili powder
    (hot if you must)
1/2 teaspoon black pepper
3/4 teaspoon salt
1/2 cup buttermilk (or just milk)
1 tablespoon vegetable shortening
2 eggs
3/4 cup yellow cornmeal
1 tablespoon all-purpose flour
1/4 teaspoon salt
1 teaspoon baking powder

In a large frying pan over medium heat break up and brown the ground meat. Add the onions and cook a minute. Add green pepper, tomato sauce, corn, chili powder, pepper and 3/4 teaspoon of the salt. Bring to a boil, reduce heat and cover. Simmer for 1 hour.

Preheat your oven to 350°F. Turn the meat mixture out into a 9-inch ungreased pie pan.

Combine the buttermilk, shortening and eggs in a bowl. Beat and add the cornmeal, flour, remaining 1/4 teaspoon salt and baking powder. Blend until smooth and pour over the meat in the pan.

Bake in the oven for 20 minutes until a toothpick comes out clean. Serves four to six people.

NELSON SIRLOIN TIPS

One of my better experiments with the microwave oven resulted in this dish. All who tasted it insisted on having the recipe. After scribbling it down for many, I'm finally getting it into a book. Now I'll be able to suggest they buy the book. Smart, huh?

1/3 cup vegetable oil
2/3 cup fry mix of your choice (or just flour)
1 lunch-sized paper bag
salt and pepper
1 1/2 pounds sirloin steak, trimmed of all fat and cut in bite-sized pieces
1 10 1/2-ounce can French onion soup

Place a large frying pan on medium heat and add the oil. Add the frying mix or flour to the paper bag. Salt and pepper the meat and shake about a third of the meat at a time in the bag to coat with flour, and add to the frying pan. Stir until all pieces are browned. Save the remaining fry mix.

Put the can of onion soup in a 1 1/2-quart glass or microwave-safe dish, with a cover. Add 1 heaping tablespoon of reserved fry mix to the soup and stir with a fork to mix well. Add the browned meat to the dish, cover and slide into the microwave oven set on high. Cook 3 minutes, remove and stir. Cook for another 3 minutes, and still another minute if it's needed to thicken the gravy. Salt and pepper to taste.

Serves two to four people. Take the hot dish right to the table for serving.

For those of you without a microwave oven, follow the recipe right up to microwaving time. Instead slide the dish into a 350°F oven for an hour. The taste is the same.

Some might like sliced onions or mushrooms added to the dish before cooking time. Do a little experimenting yourself.

MARINATED FLANK STEAK

It was Cousin Albert who sent me a recipe for flank steak in a marinade. He had dreamed up a rather revolting combination of ingredients for his marinade. I tore the top of his recipe off, then substituted my Umbrageous Steak Sauce as the marinade. Only then would it be something I would include in my book. Sorry, Albert.

1 flank steak, beef, about 1 1/2 pounds. Trim off as much fat as possible.
1 pint Umbrageous Steak Sauce (see page 162)

Place the steak in a wide, shallow pan. Pour the steak sauce over it. Turn it several times until the steak is coated well.

Refrigerate the steak a minimum of 12 hours, 24 hours if possible. Turn the steak as often as you remember it during the marinating period.

At cooking time, drain the steak and place on a broiler pan. Slide under the broiler 6 inches from the heat. Broil 6 minutes, turn, give the other side 6 minutes. This will give you rare beef. Add time if you want it medium or well-done, although I have no idea why you would want it so.

Transfer the meat to a cutting board and let stand 5 minutes. Slice across the grain of the meat into thin slices and serve. I usually reserve the remaining marinade to serve with the meat as desired. This serves two to three people with ease.

OLAF'S SWEDISH MEATBALLS

How many men have you known who had to learn to cook to eat? After getting married(!) Ole was one and I had often wondered how it came about. I wondered right up to the time I first met his wife. She is still a strikingly beautiful woman at age sixty. And by now she can cook, too. Yet this is one of Ole's recipes. He interrupted me every time I tried to get one of hers.

3 tablespoons bread crumbs
2 teaspoons cornstarch
1 tablespoon finely chopped onions
2/3 cup heavy cream (or canned milk)
1/2 cup milk
1/2 teaspoon salt
1/2 teaspoon pepper
1 teaspoon ground nutmeg
1 pound lean ground beef
1/4 pound lean ground pork
3 tablespoons butter or margarine

In a medium-sized bowl combine bread crumbs, cornstarch, onion, cream, milk, salt, pepper and nutmeg. Mix and let stand for 15 minutes.

Add the meat and mix well. You can sparingly add extra milk if the mixture is too dry to form balls. Shape about a tablespoon of meat mixture into a small ball. Continue until you run out of mixture.

Melt the butter in the frying pan over medium heat. Add all the meatballs and fry them. Keep shaking the pan to keep the balls round. Cook until the meat is just done. Avoid overcooking.

Remove to a serving dish. Serve either hot or cold. Serves two to four.

Often I make a cream gravy in the pan in which the meatballs are cooked. It can be served with or poured over the meatballs.

THE ROYAL RIB ROAST

I have always been a lover of red meat, almost any kind available to mankind. As an Alaskan, a large percentage of my meat over the years has been moose. Yet asked my favorite meat, I have to say beef. The best is the standing rib roast. I'll take it any way I can get it, rare, medium or well-done. I've even been known to go traditional and have it with Yorkshire pudding. Fix mine like this:

1 rib roast of beef, 3 to 4 pounds
1 garlic clove
salt and pepper

Begin by rubbing the entire surface of the meat with the garlic clove. Follow this with a rub of salt and top with a grind of fresh pepper all around.

Insert a meat thermometer into the thickest part of the meat. (Buy a thermometer if you don't own one.) Be sure the end of the thermometer does not touch a bone.

Place the roast fat-side down on a rack in a shallow roasting pan. Do not cover. Slip into a 375°F preheated oven and roast.

The only clue to when the meat is done rests with the thermometer. When the inside of the meat hits 135°F you have rare beef. At 155°F you have a medium roast.

At 165°F you have a well-done roast. STOP!

Remove the roast to a cutting board or serving platter and cover loosely with foil until you are ready to carve and serve.

To serve, lay the roast on its side. As I'm right-handed, the bone should be to my left. Carefully slice the meat horizontally, using the knife and a fork to lift the slices to the plates.

This roast should amply serve six people.

NOTE: See page 196 for the Old English Yorkshire Pudding recipe. I wouldn't recommend it be used for your first roast. But sometime you'll want to try it.

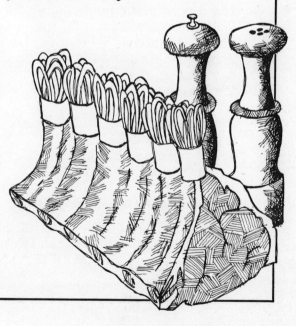

HIBROW COW IN BOURBON

In case you were beginning to wonder when the HIBROW was going to appear in the recipe section, the time has come. It is important that you approach this recipe with the proper mental attitude. It may be the only time in your life, but think, "Damn the expense!" Be brave, and if your spouse shudders as the cash register adds up the figures, think quick and mention you invited your boss to dinner.

4 tablespoons vegetable oil
8 slices white bread
2 teaspoons coarsely ground black pepper
8 3-ounce slices beef tenderloin
6 green onions, chopped fine
1/4 cup bourbon, your choice or the boss's
8 ounces butter
2 tablespoons grated Parmesan cheese
2 tablespoons grated Romano cheese
2 tablespoons fine granulated sugar
1 teaspoon salt
1/4 teaspoon each of sage, marjoram, oregano and paprika
2 4-ounce cans mushroom buttons

Heat 2 tablespoons of oil in a frying pan over medium heat. Trim the crusts from the bread slices. Fry each slice in the oil to a golden brown, turning once. Set aside on a warm plate.

Add remaining oil to the frying pan. Rub pepper into both sides of the steaks. Fry steaks 5 minutes on each side. Remove to a warm plate and set aside.

Add onions to the frying pan and sauté for 1 minute. Reduce heat to low and add bourbon to the pan. Scrape any meat residue loose from the pan and stir into the liquid. Stir in butter and when it's melted add the cheeses, stirring all the while. Add sugar, salt and seasonings. Add the mushrooms and heat to just below boiling.

On individual plate set a slice of fried bread, a round of meat and a portion of the mushroom buttons. Divide the remaining sauce between the servings and pour over the meat. Serve at once, to eight excited people. If not excited, they should be.

ALASKA BUSH BOILED DINNER

You're far out in the Bush and the last of the caribou was cooked yesterday. The Bush cook fears not, as down in the lower cupboard, far in the back, is the emergency meat. Yes, the trusty can of corned beef. The "bully beef" of the British army has found its way into another frontier. Still another creative cook is at work. Maybe this recipe.

2 cups water
1 tablespoon beef bouillon crystals
1 bay leaf
1/2 teaspoon sugar
1/2 teaspoon salt
1/4 teaspoon black pepper
2 medium potatoes, peeled and
    chunked
2 carrots, scrubbed and sliced
1 onion, chopped
2 8-ounce cans tomato sauce
1 12-ounce can corned beef, cut
    into 3/4-inch chunks

In a medium-sized pan over high heat combine water, bouillon, bay leaf, sugar, salt and pepper. When boiling, add the potatoes, carrots and onion. Cover, reduce the heat and simmer for 10 minutes. Check for tenderness of vegetables. If about done, add the tomato sauce and the cubes of corned beef. Simmer for another 4 or 5 minutes to blend flavors. Serves two to four.

If you are faced with heavy meat-eaters, add another can of corned beef. Or try the recipe using pork luncheon meat (Spam) instead of the corned beef. Use ham soup mix with the pork.

NELSON BEEF
UPSIDE-DOWN CORN BREAD

As our family grew until there were eight of us sitting around the dinner table, we fell back on some of Grandma's tricks for feeding a family. The available meat had to be stretched. This recipe could be used for just about any meat which came our way. I write it for ground beef but all too often it was ground moose, sausage, chicken or grouse. On occasion even clams and other seafoods found their way into the recipe. Try some of them as well as beef.

1 tablespoon vegetable oil
1 1/2 pounds ground beef
1 cup chopped onions
1 green pepper, chopped (optional)
1 15-ounce can tomato sauce
1 tablespoon all-purpose flour
1 teaspoon chili powder
1 teaspoon salt
1/8 teaspoon black pepper
1 cup shredded Cheddar cheese
   (optional)
1 batch Corn Bread Batter (recipe
   follows)

For this dish you will need either a 10-inch cast-iron frying pan, or a frying pan with an oven-safe handle. Heat pan over medium heat and add the oil, then break up and brown the meat. Add the onions, green pepper and tomato sauce, stir in flour and chili powder, and cook for 10 minutes while stirring. Salt and pepper to taste.

Preheat the oven to 400°F. Add the shredded cheese to the leveled meat and vegetables. Pour the Corn Bread Batter over the top. Slide the frying pan into the oven for 30 minutes. The top should feel firm. Let stand for 10 minutes and then cut and lift slices onto a serving plate. Serves six to eight.

Corn Bread Batter

In one bowl combine 2 cups cornmeal, 1 teaspoon sugar, 1/2 teaspoon salt, 1/2 teaspoon baking soda and mix well.

In a second bowl, slightly smaller, combine 1 1/2 cups of milk (buttermilk if available), 2 eggs and 3 tablespoons butter, oil or bacon drippings. Mix well and pour into a hole in the center of the cornmeal mix. Mix ingredients only until everything is just wet. Use as indicated above. Or on another day, just bake up a batch of bread without the meat recipe. Serve with butter and strawberry jam.

FRYING PAN STEW

The first time I watched a camp cook whip out a recipe like this one in a single frying pan, I was hooked. I'm a great believer in one-dish meals. They save on dish-washing, which is not one of my favorite chores. You can bet my retirement home has an automatic dish-washer. This recipe works well in camp or at home and is a favorite of one of my fellow male cooks.

1/4 cup vegetable oil
1 1/2 pounds cube steak, cut
    into 1 1/2-inch squares
1/2 teaspoon salt
1/4 teaspoon black pepper
8 small potatoes, unpeeled,
    quartered
2 garlic cloves, minced
1 red pepper, cored, seeded
    and chunked
1 green pepper, cored,
    seeded and
    chunked
1/8 teaspoon each of
    basil leaf, marjo-
    ram, rosemary leaf
2 tablespoons chopped
    fresh parsley

Add oil to a frying pan placed over high heat. Season the meat with salt and pepper and brown each piece in the hot oil. Transfer meat to a bowl and set aside.

Add potatoes to the frying pan and sauté for 1 minute. Reduce heat to medium low and continue cooking and stirring until the potatoes are browned and nearly done, about 7 minutes. Add the garlic and cook another minute. Extra oil may be added at this time if necessary.

Stir in red and green pepper chunks. Cook another 5 minutes until peppers are tender-crisp.

Return meat to the pan, sprinkle herbs over the contents. Toss to be sure everything is heated. Sprinkle the fresh parsley over the dish and take right to the table to serve four to six.

WILDMAN BEEF

As a boy I was a great fan of Edgar Rice Burroughs' books about Tarzan and other heroes. It seemed someone was always sinking pearly white teeth into raw meat. Naturally I had to have a try at raw meat. I sliced a thin piece off a roast Mother was getting ready for the oven. It wasn't at all what I had expected. Not bad, just in need of some kind of improvement. Try this recipe for the improvement:

1 pound lean sirloin steak, trimmed
    of all fat and cut in as many
    very thin slices as possible
2 egg yolks
3 teaspoons finely minced garlic
3/4 tablespoon prepared mustard
1 teaspoon salt
pepper
1 cup olive oil or vegetable oil
1/4 cup vinegar, cider- or tarragon-
    flavored
1 teaspoon Worcestershire sauce
3/4 cup grated Parmesan cheese
1 tablespoon finely chopped fresh
    parsley

Arrange slices of beef on 4 plates. Lay the meat flat and do not overlap the slices. A fan shape is nice.

Combine egg yolks, garlic, mustard, salt and a few grinds of black pepper in your blender.

In a small bowl combine oil, vinegar and Worcestershire sauce. Mix and pour slowly into the running blender. Keep pouring and blending until the contents reach the consistency of mayonnaise. Carefully stir 1/2 cup of Parmesan cheese into the mixture with a spoon.

Pour sauce across the meeting points of the fanned-out meat, dividing equally. Combine remaining Parmesan cheese and chopped parsley and sprinkle across the center of the plate. Serves four.

CHAPTER 2

LOWBROW CHICKEN

There. I've just used up the chance to make this chapter title into another book title somewhere down the trail. But not to worry. I have profound confidence in you out there to provide me with a new title when the need arises.

I doubt that a chicken should be classified as lowbrow. It's the single creature to be invited into homes all over the world, maybe not as an honored guest, but one that's always appreciated. It is found in the cooking pots of both rich and poor, and as the poor always outnumber the rich, I suppose I'll have to consider the chicken lowbrow.

The delicate flesh of the chicken, if the bird has not been run to death, can be made into a dish to tantalize the palate of a king, or even a congressman. This thought always reminds me of Ed Trilly, a true chicken-lover, and his theory. I've heard Ed, with little or no encourage-

ment, expound his theory about chicken, which is that the tenderest chicken is one that has been frightened to death. How he arrived at this theory is a story in itself.

Ed's great love for chickens and their by-products led him to establish a chicken coop on his homestead. No sooner had he installed his flock than he had a visitor. Vixen adopted him. She was the fox-type vixen, not the shrewish-type woman mentioned in the dictionary. Ed wasn't married, either.

As soon as Vixen discovered Ed's chicken coop she culled out two unproductive hens. Ed didn't even miss them at first. Who counts chickens?

Several nights later Ed awoke to a loud commotion in the henhouse. He ran out in his long-handled red underwear, shotgun in hand, aiming to kill anything that tried to get his chickens.

He was too late. Vixen had departed. A few loose feathers and a spot or two of blood testified to her visit. The remaining chickens were huddled together high on their perch, except for one. She was hanging upside down, dead. She had no mark on her, so Ed assumed she had been frightened to death.

While plucking the dead chicken, Ed confirmed that she had not suffered bodily injury. Never mind that her coopmates might have smothered her. She proved to be the tenderest chicken Ed had ever eaten, and so the Trilly theory was born.

Two nights later Vixen struck again, took two chickens, and left a third dead of fright. The thought that excitement alone might have killed the chicken never crossed his mind. This chicken too was tender, and Ed's theory was confirmed.

He now turned his attention to eliminating the chicken thief. He set traps all around the coop. Vixen didn't return for two or three nights, so Ed assumed that, being smart as foxes are alleged to be, she had moved on. Then one morning he found a dead fox pup in one of the traps, and Vixen cowering inside a live trap. As he stooped to kill her a thought hit him. "She no doubt has several more pups, waiting for her to return with one of my chickens!"

Just then a sound much like a whimper drew Ed's eyes to the brush behind his chicken coop. There crouched a pair of fox pups, waiting for their mother. He hesitated. His temper cooled and he said to Vixen, "All right, I'll let you go to your pups if you promise never to raid my chicken coop again. Do we have a deal?"

She looked up into his eyes and stood up, ready to slip from the trap when the door was opened. Ed took this for agreement, so opened the door. Vixen was out in a flash. She stopped beside her pups and looked back over her shoulder. "Remember our deal!" Ed yelled.

Ed always finished this story with, "She kept her promise, too. And you know, I didn't find another tender bird in the whole flock!"

In Alaska we have a couple of resident game birds. The state bird is pronounced *tarmigan* although it has a *p* in front of it. Don't ask me why. The other is the grouse, or spruce hen, or fool hen, depending upon who's talking about it. Both birds qualify as lowbrow chicken. The ptarmigan is the better eating, and my mouth waters when someone says "ptarmigan stew." The fool hen is edible, and stupid enough to be killed with a stick. This attribute, negative from the bird's-eye view, has made the fool hen a lifesaver to many a weary man who's been caught in the Bush without food and a gun, or out of ammunition. She's God's gift of an emergency meal.

I have seldom been lost in the woods. I use the word *seldom* because there's one man out there who knows that on one occasion I became slightly turned around. This admission will save him the trouble of writing to correct me. (Don't you hate being watched so closely?)

I have had occasion to consume an emergency bird in rather primitive circumstances. It was nearly dark when a spruce hen exploded from under my feet, scaring me out of two years' growth. Yet I marked her flight to a nearby tree, where she sat waiting. My .22 revolver's front sight disappeared in the dark foliage behind her, so I estimated where the hen's head should be. As I fired she ducked, and I missed. We went through this silly routine twice more. On my fourth try she lifted her head, no doubt to see what was going on, and found the bullet. I had dinner in hand, so I elected to camp out.

A bit of fire on a gravel beach beside a creek, and the smell of roasting bird seemed to fill the surrounding air. I ate every last scrap of that bird à la stick, and licked the bones clean. I said my thanks to Him for the meal, and added a suggestion: the size of the emergency bird should be increased, as we men have become larger and hungrier since the bird was originally designed.

You have the privilege of choosing the size of the lowbrow chicken you use in these recipes. Have fun!

TONETTE'S CHICKEN AND DUMPLINGS

Way back in the distant past my mother operated a restaurant in Cordova, Alaska, called Tonette's. One of the favorite dishes served there was chicken and dumplings. This is about as close as I can come to recreating her recipe reduced to family size.

1 chicken fryer, about 3 pounds
1/2 teaspoon salt
1/8 teaspoon black pepper
1 bay leaf
1/2 teaspoon rubbed sage

Place the chicken in a deep pot and cover with water. Add salt, pepper and herbs. Bring to a boil over high heat, reduce heat to simmer and cook for 1 hour and 15 minutes. Remove chicken, cool, debone and reserve the meat. Take out 2 cups of liquid and set aside. Return the remainder of the liquid to the stove.

Dumpling Batter

1 cup all-purpose flour
2 teaspoons baking powder
1 teaspoon salt
2 tablespoons melted butter or
    margarine
1 egg, beaten
1/4 cup minced onions
1/2 cup bread crumbs
1/2 cup milk (more if needed)

Sift together flour, baking powder, and salt. Mix in butter, egg, onions and bread crumbs. Add milk, but only enough to form a very stiff dough.

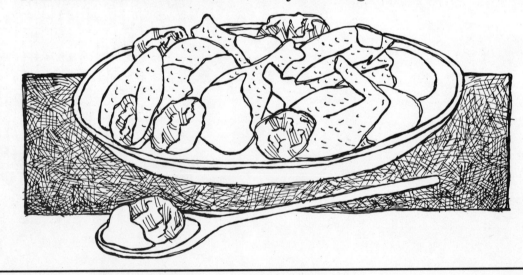

Gravy

3 tablespoons melted butter or
*   margarine*
2 cups chicken stock (saved above)
4 tablespoons flour
2 cups milk

In a separate saucepan over medium heat beat the butter into chicken stock. Add flour and milk and whisk over the heat until gravy is smooth and thick.

Now we start putting things together. Bring the original pot with chicken stock to a boil. Slip rounded tablespoonfuls of batter into the liquid. With the spoon all the way into the liquid the batter will slip off easily. When all the batter is in the pot, cover and reduce heat. Simmer for 20 minutes.

Stir the gravy into the pot. Return chicken pieces to the pot and heat everything until hot. I recommend serving right from the pot so the dumplings suffer the minimum transfer damage. Serves eight lucky people.

MARION'S MAGIC CHICKEN

With three cookbooks floating around out there, I am always getting letters from people who enclose recipes. This is one such offering. Marion had to be kidding about the magic. Still, it was interesting to try.

1 frying chicken, cut into pieces
1 cup plain yogurt
2 1/2 tablespoons mild chili
*   powder*
1 teaspoon ground coriander
2 teaspoons gingerroot, finely
*   minced (or 1 teaspoon ginger*
*   powder)*
1/4 cup lime juice (bottled okay)
1/4 teaspoon salt

The wild part begins with removal of the skin from all parts of the chicken.

Next, combine all ingredients except chicken in a bowl. Mix well and add the chicken pieces, turning so each piece is covered with the marinade. Refrigerate bowl of chicken overnight.

At cooking time preheat oven to 350°F. Arrange the chicken pieces in a flat baking pan and slide it into the oven for 1 hour. You will find the chicken develops a nice red coating after baking.

When you serve this dish to four people it will disappear rapidly. "Like magic!" Marion says.

TENNESSEE WHISKEY CHICKEN

I'll have to admit there was a time in my life when the very idea of doing anything with Tennessee whiskey except drink it was unthinkable. I've mellowed and now drink in such moderation I can even taste the fantastic flavor of one of mankind's greatest achievements. So throw a little flavor into your cooking.

6 chicken breasts, halved, deboned,
    skinned, and sliced into
    1/2-inch slices
1 teaspoon salt
1/4 teaspoon black pepper
1 teaspoon curry powder
1/4 teaspoon garlic powder
1 cup all-purpose flour
1 4-ounce cube butter
2 4-ounce cans mushrooms
1 lemon
1/4 cup Tennessee whiskey
1 1/2 cups chicken stock (bouillon
    and water)
1 tablespoon cornstarch

Spread the chicken strips on a breadboard. Sprinkle with salt, pepper, curry powder and garlic powder. Sprinkle the flour over the meat and roll each piece around so it is well-coated.

Melt the butter in a large frying pan over medium heat. Brown each piece of chicken on all sides. Add mushrooms, the juice of the lemon and a small scraping of lemon rind. Add whiskey and simmer for 5 minutes.

In a bowl combine chicken stock and cornstarch. Pour it over chicken in the frying pan. Stir over a low heat until the mixture thickens. Taste and adjust seasoning if desired.

Serve over steamed rice. Serves four to six.

SECOND-DAY CHICKEN STIR-FRY

Over years of cooking one adopts some interesting habits, even thinking ahead. For instance, tonight after dinner I might take a frozen whole chicken out of the freezer, slip it into a pot of salted water and let it cook slowly during the evening's activities. When it's done I set it aside to cool. Before bedtime I usually bone out the chicken meat into a covered refrigerator bowl. There are so many things you can do with a bowl of cooked chicken. Here's one idea.

2 tablespoons vegetable oil
1 cup peeled and thinly sliced
    carrots
2 cups coarsely chopped broccoli
1 cup diagonally sliced celery
1 1/2 cups coarsely chopped
    onions
2 garlic cloves, minced
1 teaspoon ground or grated
    ginger, fresh if
    possible
1 cup coarsely shredded
    cabbage
2 cups cooked and diced
    chicken
1 cup water
1 tablespoon cornstarch

2 tablespoons soy sauce
1 teaspoon chicken bouillon
    crystals
1/2 teaspoon salt

Set out your electric wok and turn it to medium heat. Add oil and carrots; stir for 3 minutes. Add broccoli, celery, onions, garlic and ginger. Stir-fry another 4 minutes. Add the cabbage and chicken and stir-fry 1 more minute, until the cabbage just softens.

In a small bowl combine water and cornstarch. Mix well and add soy sauce, bouillon crystals and salt. Pour the mixture over vegetables in the wok. Bring the liquid to a boil and simmer for 1 minute. Serve over hot steamed rice. Serves four.

SECOND-DAY CHICKEN BRUNCH

If the chicken you cooked and boned yesterday was truly a big chicken, use the remaining meat in a winning brunch dish, chicken hash. Try it some Sunday about noon, after sleeping in most of the morning.

2 tablespoons butter or margarine
1/2 cup minced onions
1/4 cup all-purpose flour
1/8 teaspoon seasoned salt
1/8 teaspoon cayenne pepper
1/8 teaspoon black pepper
2 cups chicken stock (saved from
  boiling chicken yesterday, or
  chicken bouillon and water)
3 1/3 cups chicken, cooked, boned
  and diced into small pieces

In a frying pan over medium heat melt butter and sauté the onions until soft. Add flour, seasoned salt, cayenne and pepper and blend. Slowly add the chicken stock and cook for 3 to 5 minutes, until the mixture is smooth and thick. Add diced chicken and reduce the heat to warm.

You have the hash ready, so now comes the decision about what to serve it over. The easiest approach is toast. A slice of toast covered with hash is great, but hash is also good over pancakes, or I've been fancy and served it over squares of fresh cornbread. That earned raves and requests for seconds. Serves two to four.

CONCORD POACHED CHICKEN

Here on the street where I live, Concord Court, there is a battle going on. No, not a revolution like way back when, but a food battle. Making and testing recipes for the creation of cookbooks represents the challenging force. My vain attempts at diet cooking make a feeble effort to hold back the forces of FAT. This is one of my dieting weapons.

2 cups chicken stock (chicken crystals and water)
1/2 cup dry white wine
1 pinch black pepper
1/4 teaspoon salt
4 chicken breast halves, deboned and skinned
1 4-ounce can mushrooms
1 envelope Butter Buds
2 tablespoons chopped onions

In a shallow bowl combine chicken stock, wine, pepper and salt (skip salt if you're off the stuff). Add chicken breasts and marinate for an hour.

Remove chicken and set aside. Pour the liquid into a saucepan over medium heat. Bring to a boil; add chicken pieces and simmer gently for 5 minutes. Remove from heat and allow the chicken to steep in the covered pan for 45 minutes. Remove chicken and keep it warm.

Reduce liquid in the pan to 1/2 cup. Discard the remainder. Add Butter Buds to the liquid and whip to mix well. Add onions and mushrooms and let the sauce heat to just under a boil.

Slice the breasts crosswise and arrange on a serving plate. Pour hot sauce over the chicken and serve. Serves two. You have all the taste and few of the calories.

WINTERTIME OVEN-BARBECUED CHICKEN

When the Matanuska wind is whistling past at sixty knots, piling snow in spots in our backyard, I get hungry. So I pull the drapes or close my eyes and think of summer. Add barbecued chicken to the fantasy and everything is great. Try this one:

2 chicken broilers, or fryers, cut up
1 tablespoon butter or margarine
1 cup chopped onions
1 cup catsup
1/2 cup vinegar
3 tablespoons brown sugar
1/4 teaspoon pepper

Preheat oven to 375°F. Scatter the chicken pieces around a rack in a shallow roasting pan. Bake for 30 minutes.

While waiting, combine butter and onions in a frying pan over medium heat. Sauté until a golden brown, about 5 minutes. Add catsup, vinegar, brown sugar and pepper to the frying pan. Bring to a boil and reduce the heat to simmer for 5 minutes.

Remove chicken from the oven. Spoon half the sauce over chicken and return it to the oven for another 15 minutes.

Remove chicken from the oven. Turn pieces over and add remaining sauce to them. Return to oven for another 15 minutes.

Now increase the temperature to 425°F for 10 minutes. Remove and serve to four to six hungry people.

EGEGIK CHICKEN STUFF

For every dozen chickens you see in the market, there are a dozen chicken livers available somewhere. No one throws away any part of a chicken that's edible. I even go in the stores and ask for chicken livers. Really! I love them fried up with lots of onions and a crumbling of bacon.

When I was an Alaska State Trooper sergeant, I arrived in Egegik on the same plane as thirty pounds of chicken livers, which came in by mistake. As a public service, I suggested several ways of cooking the mistake. I was lucky to get out of town on the same plane which brought the livers.

Try this ultimate recipe for chicken livers. It was named after my short visit to the village.

1/2 pound chicken fat, rendered into 8 tablespoons of liquid (or substitute one 4-ounce cube of butter)
1/4 cup finely minced onions
1 pound chicken livers, as fresh as possible
2 cups finely chopped onions
3 eggs, hard-cooked and finely chopped
1 1/2 teaspoons salt
1/4 teaspoon black pepper
lettuce

Over a low heat melt fat or butter in a frying pan. Add 1/4 cup minced onions.

Arrange livers on a broiling rack and broil about 4 inches from the flame for 4 to 5 minutes. All redness should be gone from the livers. Remove to chopping board and chop fine.

Add remaining onions to the frying pan and sauté for 5 minutes over medium heat. Add chopped eggs, the chopped livers and salt and pepper. Stir to mix and remove from the heat. Pour into a bowl, level the mixture and place in the refrigerator for at least 2 hours.

To serve, turn the bowl's contents out on a bed of lettuce. It can be eaten as a spread on almost anything. I've served it with crackers, bread quarters, celery, Rye Krisps, and other diet-type crackers. I find I can eat it like pudding in a bowl. Yes I was the guy who had to leave Egegik!

WORLD SERIES CHICKEN

Here in Alaska we are now receiving our television live, and with the time differential between the East Coast and us, the games interfere with getting dinner. I found and developed a recipe that lets me cook after today's game and eat tomorrow during the next game. It's almost good enough to distract a man from the game. (I did say almost.) The recipe also works for football, hockey and basketball. I have never tried it on soccer.

4 cups water
2 chicken fryers, cut up
6 chicken thighs (for dark-meat lovers)
1 cup chopped onions
1 cup thinly sliced carrots
1 celery stick, thinly sliced
2 teaspoons dry, crumbled parsley
2 whole cloves
1 bay leaf
1 teaspoon salt
1/4 teaspoon black pepper
3 cups bread crumbs, white
2 cups shelled walnuts
1 tablespoon lemon juice
1/2 teaspoon paprika

In a large pot over medium heat combine water, chicken, onions, carrots, celery, parsley, cloves, bay leaf, salt and pepper. Bring to boil and simmer for about an hour, until the chicken is tender. Set aside to cool. When cool, remove chicken and set aside in another dish.

Skim fat from top of the cooking liquid. Strain the liquid, saving the vegetables for later. Return strained liquid to the original pot and place on high heat. Boil until liquid is reduced by half.

Remove skin and bones from the chicken and cut the meat into strips and chunks. Set aside again.

Soak bread crumbs in 1/2 cup of cooking liquid. Add remaining liquid to blender. Add reserved vegetables and walnuts and blend. Add the bread crumbs and blend until you have a smooth gravy. Use additional liquid if necessary. Season to taste with lemon juice.

Combine chicken and half of the gravy in a bowl and turn out on a serving plate. Pour remaining gravy over the meat, cover and refrigerate overnight.

An hour or so before you wish to serve, take the dish from the refrigerator and sprinkle with paprika. Serve at nearly room temperature. Should serve up to ten people, with a few other extras. It tastes good with beer!

CHAPTER 3

HIBROW SOW

Sara, the moose, may well have been the Hibrow Cow of all time. She lived in the woods behind Hal Benton's cabin. Hal liked to call his bit of land, near the headwaters of the Susitna River, a farm. He would point with pride to his fifty-by-a-hundred-foot garden and then, to reinforce the idea of a farm, point out the pigpen for your visual exploration, for there was Hal's token farm animal, Mildred, the sow.

In the fall, when the weather turned cold, Mildred's lack of fur presented a problem. She was chilly. Hal offered her space in his cabin, and Mildred became a hibrow sow. She was some company for Hal during the short, cold winter days. He talked to her often, though he got only an occasional grunt in reply.

As winter progressed Hal usually began to suffer the Alaskan malady called cabin fever. Those short, cold hours of daylight and the endless nights kept him in his cabin like a man in solitary confinement. Having Mildred to talk to saved him from talking to himself. In time she learned to grunt every time Hal ended a sentence with a recognizable period. It was almost as if she understood. If the grunt was shorter or nastier than usual, it could raise Hal's blood pressure ten points. He was skidding along on the edge of stir-crazy.

Hal would take his frustrations outside during the short daylight hours and discuss Mildred's annoying behavior with Sara. It is doubtful whether she understood, but she was a good listener and she didn't grunt or snort, but she would smile. She'd just stand there chewing her willow branches, and smile. In time the smile got irritating. One more of them, Hal told her, and she'd become moose meat.

During the first week of February, a fierce storm sent both Sara and Hal seeking shelter. Inside the cabin, Hal listened as the wind tried to tear the dwelling apart, but he had built well. Two days of listening to the wind and Mildred's grunting, and Hal was thinking of silencing one of the two. A craving for roast pork came over him.

Then out of the darkness came the sound of an aircraft engine overhead. Some pilot was in deep trouble, perhaps lost away up here close to the mountains. Hal lifted himself out of his comfortable chair, slipped into winter gear including his heavy wolf-skin mittens, and stood on the porch. There, somewhat sheltered by the long overhang of the roof, he tried to place the aircraft's position. It seemed the pilot might have seen his lighted cabin window and was circling. Now the plane seemed to be in the south, over the lake. Maybe it would touch down and he'd have some company for a while — someone who could really talk.

His hope was short-lived. The engine noise was getting louder and closer. The pilot was aiming right at the lighted window beside the door. Hal leaped off the porch, took two running jumps, and landed with his head buried in snow. Later he described what he heard as "the tearing metal and splintering wood, and then the 'whomp' of a gasoline fire."

Seconds later he was on his feet, staring back at the raging fire that had been his home. Already the roof was gone, but the shell of tough logs was like a wall around a solid mass of flames. He moved away to escape the heat, and was halfway around the cabin when the screaming started. It came from behind the cabin, and he knew it wasn't Mildred.

Some twenty feet from the back wall of the burning cabin lay a parka-clad figure. The ridgepole from the cabin lay across the figure, fire was creeping up the ridgepole, and the surrounding snow was steaming from the heat. Hal waded through the snow to the end of the ridgepole that wasn't aflame, and lifted it off the figure. Then he grabbed the upthrust arms and pulled the person a safe distance from the fire.

Once safe, he rolled the figure over and found himself looking down at Mary Gilbertson, the Public Health Nurse from McGrath.

Her eyes were closed but she was breathing. As he bent closer her eyes fluttered open, and then her mouth, and she emitted a terrible scream right in his face.

"Shut up, Mary!" Hal ordered.

Her throat worked a couple of times and she finally said, "What happened?"

"You just flew your plane into my cabin."

"The fire?"

"Both your plane and my cabin."

"All I remember is suddenly being too close to the ground, a windshield full of trees, and then I saw a light and was trying to figure out where I was. I woke up to flames, and you can guess where I thought I was."

"Hell."

"Yes, and Satan bending over me. We're in trouble, huh?"

"Got emergency gear in the cache over there," he said, and began dragging her toward the cache. "You're always in danger of fire out here."

She was hurting, and when he finally got her settled in a huge down sleeping bag under the cache, she lay there trembling from the cold and shock. He knew she needed extra heat to survive, and in spite of all the heat going to waste at the cabin, body heat was all he had to offer. He slipped off his parka and slid down into the bag beside her.

Some time later she came back from either sleep or unconsciousness. "Hal," she said, "I'm warm now, but I'm certainly not comfortable."

"You were by far the coldest woman I ever went to bed with," Hal said with a grin.

"If that's a pass, forget it. What's your altitude here?"

"I'd guess nine hundred feet. Did you file a flight plan?"

"Yes, but not to here!"

"They'll search."

"We'll just have to wait, huh?"

The dim light of dawn revealed a scene of destruction. Not much was left of the cabin, nor the plane, but the smell of roast pork drifted to Hal on the light wind. He slipped out of the sleeping bag and found some sections of the corrugated iron roof with which he managed to bridge the hot ground and reach Mildred's remains. A man in trouble can't pass up any source of food, after all. He carved off a generous chunk of roast pork. Mary wouldn't touch it, so he set her part aside to freeze for later use. She just snuggled close to his warmth and went back to sleep.

Two days later came the *whop whop whop* of an approaching helicopter. Hal slipped out of the bag and flagged down the pilot to his garden patch. Mary was very weak, but they bundled her into the craft and flew straight to the hospital in Anchorage. In six months she was back flying her rounds in the Bush. She was a determined woman.

The news value of the story faded rapidly, but negotiations with the insurance company went on. Mary's company wanted to make a cash settlement. Hal wanted a new cabin built on his farm. They compromised on a sectional cabin built in Anchorage and flown out to be assembled on the site. Hal agreed to have the event filmed for a commercial.

If you saw the commercial you no doubt saw Sara, the hibrow moose cow. She watched the proceedings with great interest, chewing her willow branches and smiling. She was a great distraction to the cameramen.

Mildred the hibrow sow was not in the commercial as most of her was already in Hal, to be remembered, as most porkers are, only by those who have fed on them, and then only if a close friendship had existed between them.

As you can see by this story, pork is good eating. It doesn't matter where you find it, but these recipes I'm offering may suit you better than Hal and Mary's method of cooking.

49/50
PORK ROAST

We of this North Country are well aware that Alaska was the 49th state admitted to the United States. Hawaii was the 50th. I admit that more Alaskans go to Hawaii to help them celebrate than vice versa. The major flow of people southward coincides with the shortening days of our winter. All seem to come back raving about the pork they tasted in our sister state. I haven't been there yet, so I just cook it this way and fantasize a bit. Hey! This book might make my escape possible next winter. Meanwhile try this recipe:

4-pound pork butt roast
2 tablespoons salt
4 tablespoons liquid smoke
aluminum foil

Lay roast on a cutting board and score the side about 1/4 inch deep and 1 inch apart. Rub meat with salt and liquid smoke. Wrap tightly in heavy aluminum foil.

Place wrapped roast on a rack in a roasting pan. Slide into a pre-heated 500°F oven. Roast for 45 minutes. Reduce temperature to 250°F and roast 3 hours.

Remove and unwrap carefully. The meat will be falling-apart tender. It can be shredded for serving. Serves up to eight.

EDNA'S PORK ROAST

Edna is one of the finest cooks I have ever met. To herself she is just a housewife. To me she is Chef Edna. Of course there are a lot of people who just call her Grandma, and look forward to her wonderful meals. It seems there are more of those people every nine months or so. Fertility is a by-product of good nutrition.

1/2 cube (2 ounces) butter or
    margarine
1/3 cup finely chopped onions
1/3 cup finely chopped celery
1/3 cup finely chopped green
    pepper
2 cloves garlic, finely minced
1 1/4 teaspoons salt
1/2 teaspoon black pepper
1 teaspoon paprika
1 teaspoon thyme
1/2 teaspoon dry mustard
1 3-pound pork roast, boneless loin

In a frying pan over medium heat, melt the butter and sauté the onions, celery, green pepper and garlic. When they're limp, add the seasonings and cook for 4 minutes. Set aside to cool.

Place the roast on a cutting board, fat side up. Cut several slits along the top, almost through to the meat. Pack each slit full of vegetable mixture. Transfer roast to a roasting pan, still fat side up. Insert a roasting thermometer where roast is the thickest, without touching a bone. Roast in a preheated 325°F oven for about 2 hours. The internal temperature should reach 170°F, as pork should be served well-done.

Remove to a cutting board and slice. Serves up to six.

BUSH COUNTRY EMERGENCY DINNER

We who live in Alaska's far-distant places have always liked to give the impression that we live off the land. Moose for dinner every other night, alternated with wonderful fish or shellfish dinners. We do enjoy a lot of good foods, grown on the land and in the waters, yet very few folks come close to living off the land. All too often, here and there, emergencies arise. With nothing shot or caught for dinner, one can only reach down into the cupboard to bring out an old standby. The Army brought pork luncheon meat to us, and we remember. Yes, the very Spam we soldiers swore to hate into eternity. Add it to some of our tender home-grown cabbage and you have a meal.

1 can pork luncheon meat (Spam, or choose your brand)
1 teaspoon vegetable oil
1 head cabbage, about 2 pounds, coarsely shredded
1 tablespoon soy sauce
1/4 teaspoon salt
1/4 teaspoon black pepper

Cut meat into chunks, about bite-sized. Add oil to a frying pan with a cover. Cook meat over medium heat for 2 to 3 minutes. Add cabbage and cook another 5 minutes, stirring occasionally. Add soy sauce and other seasonings and mix well. Cover pan and cook another few minutes at a simmer. When the cabbage is done to your liking, the dish is finished.

Serves two to four.

SUSITNA SCRAPPLE

Off to the north of my Matanuska Valley is the Susitna River in its valley. On a homestead in that valley I was first served this dish. After some conniving, convincing and downright rearranging of the truth, I came away with this recipe. Anything to get you the best recipe.

12 cups pork stock, or ham bouillon and water
2 cups cooked pork, cut into small pieces
3 cups cornmeal
1 medium onion, chopped
1 teaspoon ground marjoram
1 teaspoon crumbled sage
1 teaspoon ground thyme
salt and pepper

In a large pan over medium heat combine stock, pork, cornmeal, onion, herbs and salt and pepper to taste. Bring to boil and then simmer for 1 hour.

Remove from heat and pour contents into 2 large loaf pans, dividing equally. Chill the mixture until it sets. Refrigerate until needed.

To serve, turn the loaf onto a cutting board and cut in slices about 1/2 inch thick. Sauté the slices in butter in a frying pan over medium heat. Serve with hot syrup. Serves six to eight.

Or you can serve the slices cold with your favorite topping. Some like it with catsup, applesauce or chocolate syrup. Use your imagination as well.

CAMP TEN
PORK CHOPS

I first tasted these pork chops in our tenth camp one summer while I was in a crew surveying the Kenai Peninsula, way back in the summer of 1939. The cook had lost track of the number of camps, meals and days. Lemon extract was his problem. He didn't flavor with it, he drank it. He could still cook, and he didn't have bad breath unless you didn't like the odor of lemons.

As you see, the recipe has been reduced. Feel free to increase it to serve your crew.

2 tablespoons vegetable oil
4 pork chops, as lean as possible
1 cup applesauce
1/2 cup sherry wine (my addition)
1 teaspoon ground tarragon
1 teaspoon ground ginger
1 8-ounce can mushrooms
1 tablespoon soy sauce

Add oil to a large frying pan over medium heat. Add the chops and fry 5 minutes on each side. They should be well-browned.

Combine applesauce, wine, herbs, mushrooms and soy sauce in a bowl. Mix well and pour mixture over chops in the pan. Cover, reduce heat and cook for 20 minutes. Check for tenderness and cook longer if necessary.

Serves two to four. I suggest serving these chops with rice, as it would be a shame to waste all that fantastic sauce.

TIMBERLINE PORK

I had had sweet and sour pork only in a Chinese restaurant until we let Jerry take over the cooking on a hunting trip in Southeastern Alaska. It is true our hunting camp was a sizeable boat anchored in a quiet harbor, so Jerry had the advantage of an excellent gas range on which to cook. The older I get, the more I like camping aboard ships or in RVs. This is living and eating well.

1 tablespoon vegetable oil
1 pound boneless pork cut in
   3/4- inch chunks
1 large can pineapple chunks
   and juice
1/3 cup cider vinegar
1/2 teaspoon salt
1 1/2 teaspoons garlic powder
2 tablespoons sugar
1 green pepper, chunked
   (my addition)
1 tomato, sliced (also my addition)
1 teaspoon cornstarch

Add oil and pork chunks to a frying pan over medium heat. Brown the pork well and pour off any fat.

Drain juice from the pineapple into a measuring cup. Add enough water to make 1 cup. Add 1/4 cup vinegar, salt, garlic powder and sugar. Mix well and pour over the pork. Cover the pan and cook over low heat for 30 minutes, or until the meat is tender.

Add pineapple chunks, green pepper and tomato. Combine remaining vinegar and cornstarch, mix well and add to the pan. Cook until everything is warm and the sauce thickens slightly. Turn out into a serving dish. Serves two to four.

Again I recommend serving the dish with rice, noodles, or even spaghetti.

NOTE: If you ever get that mountain sheep, try this recipe using its meat. Wow! Or try the recipe with the old standby, chicken. (Adjustments necessary.)

MIDWINTER PORK ROAST

In this land of the summertime midnight sun we have the opposite as well, the day of hardly any daylight. It gets down to just a little more than three hours of the bright stuff. When that shortest day has come and gone and the days get longer minute by minute, many of us celebrate. My friend Tom, who has eaten moose and caribou for the first half of the winter, celebrates with a special dinner. Connie and I were invited to one such dinner. This is what was served:

2-pound pork roast, loin with bones
1/2 teaspoon salt
1/2 teaspoon pepper
1/2 teaspoon paprika
1 cup apple cider with no sugar
    added
1 cup beef stock (bouillon and water)
1 cup canned evaporated milk
4 tablespoons margarine
2 4-ounce cans mushrooms
2 apples, cored, peeled and sliced
    into eighths (prepare just
    before using)

Season the roast with salt, pepper and paprika. Place on a roasting rack in a heavy roaster pan. Insert the meat thermometer without touching a bone. Slide into a preheated 450°F oven for 35 minutes, or until the thermometer reads 165°F. Remove to a platter and keep warm.

Discard any drippings from the roasting pan and wipe clean. Add apple cider to the pan and place over high heat. Boil to reduce cider by one-half. Add stock and milk. Cook over low heat for 15 minutes until the mixture has slightly thickened; pour into a bowl and keep warm.

In a saucepan add 2 tablespoons of margarine over low heat. Sauté mushrooms slightly and add to the sauce bowl. Add remaining margarine and lightly sauté apple slices until they are golden in color.

Carve the roast into 4 serving-size pieces. Divide sauce among the servings. Place pork roast on 4 dinner plates and surround each section of meat with golden apple slices. Serve to four.

PALMER PORK ROAST AND CABBAGE

The farmers here in the Matanuska Valley have long had a contest to see who could grow the largest cabbage by State Fair time. The champion cabbage is well over 75 pounds and growing larger every year. Personally, I grow the smaller variety and eat them sooner. Quite a number of them fell victim to this recipe last summer, and I'm back plotting against others for this coming summer. This is a start today and eat tomorrow recipe.

4-pound pork rolled roast
3 cups apple cider
1 cup cider vinegar
4 teaspoons margarine
1 cup chopped onions
1 green cabbage, cut in wedges

Start today by placing roast in a dish that will fit into the refrigerator. Pour over it 3 tablespoons of cider and 3 tablespoons of vinegar. Roll roast around to be sure all parts are exposed to the marinade. Slide into refrigerator and turn roast in the marinade as many times as you remember in the next 24 hours.

The next day, preheat the oven to 475°F and place roast on a rack in a roasting pan. Insert meat thermometer. Put roast in the oven for 15 minutes. Reduce temperature to 350°F and roast for another 35 minutes. Baste meat with marinade several times during these steps. When the interior temperature of the meat reaches 170°F, remove from oven and let it rest.

During roasting time you can be preparing the sauce. In a frying pan over medium heat sauté onions in margarine until browned, about 5 minutes. Add 1 1/2 cups of cider and 1/4 cup of vinegar to onions. Boil until reduced to half. Keep sauce warm.

In a covered pan or skillet, arrange cabbage sections. Pour remaining cider and vinegar over cabbage. Cover and steam over medium heat for 30 minutes, or until cabbage is tender.

To serve, slice the meat and arrange on a serving platter. Surround with cabbage wedges and pour sauce over the meat. Serves six to eight.

THREE-WAY PORK RIBS

I am sure there are hundreds of ways to prepare ribs. I have tasted them done in dozens of ways and I anticipate tasting many more. Something else to live for. I dearly love ribs. Here are a few ideas you might like to try.

4 pounds pork ribs, separated into individual ribs
salt and pepper

Preheat oven to 400°F. Salt and pepper ribs to your taste. Place on a rack in a roasting pan. Roast for 45 minutes. Meanwhile, choose your glaze and get it ready.

Apricot Glaze

1 10- to 12-ounce jar apricot preserves
1/2 cup Dijon-style mustard
2 garlic cloves, finely minced

Combine the ingredients in a small saucepan over medium heat. Cook 5 minutes or until it's a syrupy mixture. Brush glaze on the individual ribs, turning as necessary. Bake ribs another 10 minutes and glaze a second time. Bake for another 10 minutes. Remove from oven and coat one last time with any remaining glaze.

Parmesan-Soy Crust

1 cup Dijon mustard
2 tablespoons soy sauce
1 cup bread crumbs
1 teaspoon crumbled oregano
1/2 cup grated Parmesan cheese

In a small bowl combine mustard and soy sauce. In a second bowl combine bread crumbs, oregano and cheese. Brush each rib with mustard sauce, both sides, and sprinkle with the crumb mixture. Return ribs to the oven for another 20 minutes. Do not turn. Remove from oven and serve hot.

Barbecue Sauce

1 small onion, finely chopped
2 tablespoons margarine
1 8-ounce can tomato sauce
1 garlic clove, minced
1/3 cup finely chopped celery
1/3 cup water
2 tablespoons cider vinegar
2 tablespoons Worcestershire sauce
2 tablespoons brown sugar
1 teaspoon dry mustard
1 teaspoon salt
1/4 teaspoon black pepper

In a small saucepan over medium heat, sauté onions in margarine until lightly browned. Add remaining ingredients. Reduce heat and simmer 20 minutes. Stir occasionally.

While still hot, brush sauce on ribs and return to the oven for 10 minutes. Brush sauce on again and roast still another 10 minutes. Remove from oven and brush on one more layer of sauce just before serving. Enjoy!

ZUCCHINI-SEASONED PORK CHOPS

Zucchini squash grow wildly here in the Matanuska Valley, often reaching eight to ten pounds in the long summer days. I prefer to pick them small and eat them as often as possible in season. This is another quick one-pan recipe that has found favor here.

3 tablespoons all-purpose flour
5 tablespoons grated Parmesan
    cheese
1 1/2 teaspoons salt
1/4 teaspoon pepper
1/2 teaspoon paprika
1/2 teaspoon dill weed
2 tablespoons vegetable oil
6 lean pork chops
2 onions, sliced
3 zucchini squash, 6 to 8 inches,
    sliced

Combine flour, 2 tablespoons Parmesan cheese, salt, pepper, paprika and crumbled dill weed in a paper sack. Shake well.

Add oil to a frying pan over medium heat. Shake each pork chop in the paper sack to coat, then place in the frying pan and brown on both sides. When all are browned, spread slices of onion over the chops, add 1/3 cup of water, cover and let simmer for 15 minutes.

Add slices of zucchini over the layer of onions. Sprinkle remaining flour mixture and extra cheese over top. Cover and continue simmering for another 25 minutes. Do not stir.

I suggest you take the frying pan right to the table and serve from it. The dish wouldn't look so pretty after you transferred it to a serving dish. Serves three to six.

CHAPTER 4

SEAFOOD NOW

I long ago lost count of the days I've spent fishing or otherwise attempting to capture creatures of Alaska's seas. Those creatures include almost anything that swims, drifts, hops, crawls, scuttles, or digs itself into the sea floor. I'll readily admit that I have not eaten everything I have lured or strong-armed out of the sea. There are some unappetizing and even downright ugly things in our waters.

When given a choice, I have preferred to eat the best-looking creatures and leave the ugly alone. Some of the ugliest still haunt me. On the top of my ugly list has to be the Irish lord. With due respect to my Irish ancestors, I say the fish is well-named. My experience with the species has usually come about while I was fishing for halibut. The Irish lord is quicker to the bait — or more numerous down there near the bottom.

I have never had the choice of ignoring the other prolific species down there, the tom cod. This is what you usually get the second time you lower a line for halibut. As I've always thrown these two species back, I may have caught the same dumb fish many times. There's no use taking them home. Even the cat will not eat either species.

Next on my list of uglies is the shark. I have caught few over the years and mostly they were the dogfish shark, not more than four feet long. The ones that have brought my hook back to the surface were not really ugly. They are long, slinky, streamlined critters, almost handsome, maybe, if they're swimming in Marineland. But alongside the boat, showing me all those wicked teeth, they are ugly.

I remember on one occasion when I was fishing hopefully for halibut with a wire leader, up came this toothy character. He smiled at me from about half an oar-length away, bit a chunk out of the oak oar blade, and headed for the side of the boat. I snubbed him close alongside and reached for the hook disgorger. I looked again at all those teeth, so close, and at the fourteen-inch disgorger in my hand, then reached for a pair of side-cutter pliers and snipped the leader. Off he went, with a wire trinket to show the other sharks.

I'll always remember the helpful fellow on the float when I came in that night. He listened to my remarks and then said, "They *are* good to eat, you know." He tempted me, but not to try eating shark. I put my fist into my pocket and went home entertaining a fantasy of that guy crawling along the float looking for his teeth.

Then there is the sea snail. Every time I pulled my crab trap, there they would be, enjoying the bait I'd intended for crab. If the snail number was high, the crab take was usually low. Crabs aren't so dumb as to go into a trap that isn't baited. Finally I learned. I'd stuff the snails into a mesh bag, hit them with a hammer, and use them to rebait the trap. Turnabout is fair play.

After I'd been fighting snails for twenty years, someone said, "They *are* good to eat, you know." Like the French garden snail, he said, they could be turned into escargots. I was interested enough to get a recipe from the informant, and when I pulled the next trap I gathered the snails into a bucket. I studied the ugly things while I pulled the next trap, then dumped the snails from the bucket into a mesh bag and reached for the hammer. If I remember right, the recipe went into the bag with the snails. I still think it was one of my wiser decisions.

As I have written before, I have a longstanding compact with the octopus, reached on my first two contacts with members of the species. When I was a small boy aboard a shrimp boat, a baby octopus came up in the shrimp trawl, and I was challenged to get him into a bucket and throw him back into the sea. I was lucky. He went out through a scupper hole in the ship's side, and let me keep the bucket.

On my second meeting with an octopus, I was sitting in a twelve-foot aluminum skiff when I lifted the line to which he had attached himself. His arm span was wider than the skiff was long, but he let me go and I got to keep the skiff. Out of gratitude I have never fished for, caught, cooked nor eaten an octopus. As I said before, turnabout is fair play.

I suppose I must mention another creature of the deep that I have never caught, nor eaten, nor been eaten by — the common, everyday sea serpent. There! I can see it in your eyes! "Here comes the old sea-serpent legend again!" The scientific community has for hundreds of years denied the existence of these creatures. Men have been institutionalized for insisting they have been attacked by, or even laid eyes on, a sea serpent. This story is for the slim minority of sane individuals who have actually seen sea serpents.

The fact that there were sea serpents in Prince William Sound was no secret around our house. They were known by the generic name of Old Charley. Dad would say, "We saw Old Charley in the Windward Passage this trip." Mother would answer, "Charley who?" A nice, noncommittal response acceptable in any group. I was about to enter the sixth grade in Cordova when I asked Mother, "Charley who?" She said, "Go ask your father."

I did, and I saw Dad turn into The Captain. As I've said elsewhere, when he was wearing The Captain's hat, it behooved me to listen carefully. He explained that most fishermen, as they made their living on the sea, had seen sea serpents often and knew they were for real. Few landlubbers believed in sea serpents. They usually credited sea-serpent sightings to booze. "DTs of the sea," some dry-foot had quipped. So why talk about sea serpents around landlubbers?

I discussed The Captain's remarks with my buddies, those from fishing families. They knew about sea serpents, and knew enough not to discuss them with the town kids.

Then came the day aboard ship, when I was perched on the wheelhouse stool beside my older brother, who was conning the ship. Suddenly he pointed to starboard and said, "Look! Put the glasses on those dark spots!" I did. They looked like three oil drums evenly spaced, end to end and about half down in the water. "Old Charley!" Ken said. "Keep watching. He'll lift his head."

Ken turned the ship toward the spots. I'd guess we were three hundred yards from them when the third spot developed into a short neck and a head. The head swiveled and looked right at me. I had about fifteen seconds to study it through the glasses. My impression was all eyes and mouth with overtones of teeth. Then Old Charley sounded and the sighting was over. I looked at Ken in wonder.

"I suspect we have a new believer," Ken said with a grin.

"How can anyone not believe?"

"People believe what they want to believe, or what they think they're supposed to believe. Some feel that if you deny something long enough, it goes away and their beliefs become truths."

I should end the story right here, so you'd never know I wasn't so smart in my youth as I thought I was, but there's more. School started and we had a new teacher who assigned the usual what-happened-to-me-last-summer essay. I elected to write about seeing the sea serpent. I almost blew my future as a writer that day. The teacher labeled my story as fiction, told the class it was nonsense, and then made me stand up in front of the class and read it. The kids all laughed, all except those from fishing families. They looked worried. I got an F on the story. How do you grade it?

LITTLE
HALIBUT BAKE

Back in the days when I was catching chicken (small) halibut on commercial gear, I could seldom resist taking the tasty things home to dinner. Now I have the same trouble with red snapper fillets in the market. This is the recipe I blame for my problem. Try it!

6 tablespoons vegetable oil
1 teaspoon salt
1/4 teaspoon black pepper
2 pounds fish fillets, halibut, red snapper, or any other whitefish
1/2 teaspoon ground turmeric
6 tablespoons minced parsley
1/2 cup chopped onions
1 garlic clove, minced

Place 1 tablespoon of oil in a shallow baking dish large enough to contain all fillets in one layer. Salt and pepper both sides of the fillets and place them in the dish.

In a small bowl combine remaining ingredients with remaining 5 tablespoons of oil. Mix well and spread over fish fillets.

Bake in a preheated 350°F oven for 15 to 20 minutes. Baste with cooking liquid several times during the cooking time. Test with a fork for flaking to determine when done.

Serve right in the cooking dish, so the sauce will be available, to up to four people.

NOTE: I sometimes cook this dish in the microwave, which has taken over many of the cooking duties in my house. Use a shallow glass microwave dish and plastic covering, pierced once to let out steam. Or even better, use one of the specially designed microwaving dishes with a vented cover.

Cook on high for 3 minutes, turn dish one quarter around and give it another 3 minutes, another turn and 2 more minutes. Let the dish sit, covered, for at least 2 minutes before serving. If you have an automatic turntable in your microwave, skip turning by hand.

NOTE: For those of you on a low-fat diet, here is something different. Mix an envelope of Butter Buds with water and use the resulting liquid in place of the oil. Increase the liquid to oil ratios by one half. Otherwise cook the same.

SVENSEN FRIED FISH

When you have lived as long as I have, you have seen a lot of fish poorly fried. It's time to provide the world with a quick, effective way to fry fish. I liked the way Ole Svensen did it. Here's the recipe he gave me when he had demonstrated his method:

4 codfish fillets, fresh, thawed
    frozen, or Sven's favorite,
    dried and salted. Or use any
    whitefish fillets.
2 cups all-purpose flour
2 teaspoons black pepper
2 teaspoons salt (skip if you're
    using dried fish)
2 tablespoons water
2 eggs
1 cup vegetable oil (or bacon
    grease for campers and
    others living dangerously)
lemon wedges (optional)

If it is dried, salted cod fillets, you start yesterday, soaking the fillets in water for 24 hours, then go on.

With fresh or just-thawed or soaked fish the next step is to cut 2-inch slices across the fillet.

Combine flour, pepper and salt in a small bowl (skip salt with salted fish). Beat water and eggs together in a second bowl.

Take a piece of fish and dip it into egg mixture. Let it drip into the bowl for a moment or two. Roll damp fish in flour. Set the floured fish on a rack until all pieces are ready.

Heat oil in a heavy frying pan to almost smoking hot. Quickly add all fish pieces. Fry the fish until golden and crisp, turning once, or twice if necessary. The cooking time should be 4 to 6 minutes.

Serves two to four people. Lemon wedges, if you've got 'em.

NOTE: Try the So-You-Like-Garlic Sauce on page 163 with fish fried this way.

GRILLED HALIBUT FILLETS

This recipe is the outgrowth of several conditions I have found over the years. When catching small halibut and even sole, I found filleting them aboard the boat made more room for fish in the ice chest. And fresher fish when I reached home. Then I fell into the habit of not skinning the small fillets so they didn't fall apart so easily. This naturally led to not skinning the fillets before I cooked them. Enough explanation. Let's cook.

4 fish fillets, boneless but with
skin (or without skin if the
market is furnishing the fish)
1/4 cup vegetable oil
salt and pepper

Brush all fillets with oil on both sides and salt and pepper. Fire up the grill and when it is burning just right, place fillets on the grill, skin side up. Cook 3 minutes, turn and cook the other side 2 minutes. Carefully transfer fish to the serving plate.

Serves two to four depending upon appetites and size of fillets.

NOTE: Serve with your favorite fish sauce. Or try one of these: Gene's White Wine Sauce, page 161; So-You-Like-Garlic Sauce, page 163; Oriental Fish Sauce, page 158.

NELSON QUICK FISH POACH

Today I have one of those long pans called a fish-poaching pan. It was a gift from a reader who noted I mentioned in my first cookbook that I did not own one. I use it only for major fish-poaching undertakings when the family gathers at our house. It is wonderful when cooking a whole fish. Otherwise I find myself falling back to this fairly simple method:

2 cups water
3 tablespoons lemon juice
1/8 teaspoon black pepper
2 teaspoons salt
2 bay leaves
2 pounds fish fillets (any
   whitefish poaches best)

Combine everything except the fish in a frying pan over high heat. Bring liquid to a boil and slip fillets into boiling liquid.

Cook for 3 minutes, turn carefully with a spatula and cook for another 2 minutes. Test for flaking. Remove from liquid, drain and serve. Serves two, but more fish can be cooked in the same amount of liquid to serve more people.

BETTER
BAKED FISH

This recipe is right out of my wife's grandmother's cookbook. In sixty-five years in Alaska I had never heard of the method. It's well worth a try. As you can see, some changes were necessary due to supplies available.

*1 pound salt pork (I substituted
   bacon), thinly sliced*
1 whole, large fish, your choice
salt and pepper
*3 tablespoons butter or
   margarine*
3 tablespoons all-purpose flour
*1 cup buttered cracker crumbs
   (I assumed the crackers are
   buttered and then crumbled)*
*buttered paper (I substituted
   aluminum foil)*

You need a baking pan large enough to handle the size of the fish. My 5-pound salmon without head and tail fit nicely into a 10-by-17-inch flat baking pan. Line the bottom of pan with slices of salt pork or bacon. If using bacon you could salt the fish slightly. I didn't. Lay washed and dried fish on salt pork strips. Salt and pepper the up side.

In a bowl cream together butter and flour. Use half the mixture to butter the top side of the fish. Turn fish over, salt and pepper the other side and apply a coating of the butter mixture. Sprinkle cracker crumbs over upper side of the fish. Add a couple of slices of salt pork or bacon on top of the crackers.

Cover with foil (or buttered paper if you're going original) and slide pan into a preheated 350°F oven. Bake for 1 hour, and remove foil. Slide back into oven for 10 to 15 more minutes to brown top of fish.

Carefully remove entire fish to a serving platter and take it to the table for the reception it deserves. Serves four to who knows? It depends upon the size of the fish.

NOTE: I've used the recipe to do a halibut roast of about 5 pounds. The cooking time had to be extended a few minutes, but the results were worth it. Baked halibut tends to be slightly dry due to lack of fat in the flesh. This method of cooking corrected that fault.

MELODIE'S CLAM FRITTERS

As a youth living on the beaches of Alaska, I often caught and cooked crabs and clams close to where we found them. Half a five-gallon gas can was our cook pot. We even found the can on the beach and made our pots. I had long known about clam chowder, but it wasn't until I became interested in a girl that I learned about clam fritters. I only wish I had started collecting recipes earlier in life. I can name a recipe for her, Melodie. It does have a ring.

1 cup vegetable oil (or bacon grease if available)
3 eggs, slightly beaten
1/2 cup all-purpose flour
1/2 teaspoon salt
1/4 teaspoon black pepper
1/2 teaspoon garlic powder
1/2 cup chopped onions

1 teaspoon Worcestershire sauce
1 teaspoon soy sauce
1 cup clams, chopped (substitute 2 6 1/2-ounce cans of clams, drained)

Pour oil into a frying pan and set over medium heat. In a medium-sized bowl combine all the ingredients. Mix well. Drop tablespoon-sized gobs of batter into hot oil. Fry until one side is brown. Turn and brown the other side. Try for a golden brown color. Lift finished fritter and set aside. Keep warm while you finish the others.

The batch will serve from four to six depending upon how well they like clams.

There are several good seafood sauces on the market, but do try Seward Seafood Sauce, served hot.

LEFT-HANDED HALIBUT BROIL

While living in Southeastern Alaska, the land of fish galore, I became like most local residents, disdainful of the flounder. We called them left-handed halibut, because their head placement is opposite to the halibut's. You have to see them to understand. During my years in Southeast I threw back into the sea many thousand flounders. Then one day I came home from the store with what I thought was a block of frozen red snapper, only to find it was flounder. It was also thawed. So —

2 tablespoons vegetable oil
1 teaspoon soy sauce
1 teaspoon lemon juice
1/2 teaspoon ground ginger
2 garlic cloves, minced
aluminum foil
salt and pepper
1 1/2 pounds whitefish (even
*   flounder)*

In a small bowl combine oil, soy sauce, lemon juice, ginger and garlic.

Line a small baking dish with foil. Salt and pepper one side of the fish and place salted side down in the pan. Salt and pepper second side. Pour contents of the bowl over the fish.

Marinate fish in the sauce for 30 minutes, turning once.

Slide the pan with fish under the broiler about 4 inches from heat source. Broil for 2 minutes; remove and baste with liquid. Broil another 2 minutes and baste again. After a third 2-minute broiling, test the fish for flaking and doneness. Give it another 2 minutes if necessary.

Serves two to four. You don't have to tell them it's flounder. They'll never know if you don't.

SALMON STEAK BAKE

I have slipped my readers some great recipes for cooking salmon. Fish cooking is easy, because most people will eat it any way the cook serves it. They deserve better. The salmon deserves better. So I offer the following recipe.

3/4 cup soy sauce
1/4 cup sesame oil
1/4 cup dry sherry
1 tablespoon honey
1 garlic clove, minced
2 tablespoons minced onions
1 tablespoon fresh ginger, minced
4 fish steaks, king salmon
    preferred, cut 1 inch thick
1 lemon, quartered
aluminum foil

The first step is to create the marinade by combining soy sauce, sesame oil, sherry, honey, garlic, onions, and ginger in a bowl.

Place fish steaks in a shallow baking pan and pour marinade over them. Turn the fish every 15 minutes for an hour.

Cut 4 pieces of foil, each large enough to wrap 1 steak. Add a steak, 1/2 cup of marinade and the juice of a quarter of lemon to the first package. Fold foil to enclose fish and seal tightly. Do the same with each fish steak.

Lay 4 steaks in baking pan deep enough to control an accidental spill of liquid. Slide into a 400°F preheated oven. Bake for 25 to 35 minutes.

Remove from the oven and place a steak package on a plate, open carefully and serve with the foil folded back just enough to expose the steak in all its glory, complete with its own supply of sauce. Do the same with the remaining 3 packages.

Serves four people amply. If they don't claim you are the best chef in Alaska, don't invite 'em back. I'll be glad to take one of their places next time around. Enjoy!

LEFTOVER FISH FOR TWO

With a large family of eight to feed for so many years it was hard to start cutting back on amounts as we were being reduced to two, Connie and me. Every once in a while I still end up with a platter of leftover stuff in the refrigerator. Sometimes even fish. Connie knows what we'll have the next day. Yep! this is it. I love it.

2 cups fish, whatever available
    (or open a 16-ounce can in
    case of emergency)
2 bread slices, toasted and
    blended to crumbs
1 4-ounce can mushroom pieces
    and stems
1 tablespoon dry parsley,
    crumbled
1 tablespoon chives, minced
    or dry
2 garlic cloves, minced
2 tablespoons mayonnaise
salt and pepper
3 tablespoons vegetable oil
1/3 cup dry, nonfat, instant milk
1 tablespoon onion powder

Crumble fish in a large bowl, add bread crumbs, mushrooms, parsley, chives, garlic, and mayonnaise. Salt and pepper to taste and mix well. You can add just a little water if the mix is too dry to form into balls. Divide mixture into 4 even-sized balls. Flatten the balls into patties.

In a frying pan over medium heat bring the oil up to cooking temperature.

Combine powdered milk and onion powder in a shallow bowl. Dip each fish patty into the mixture, turn, and dip the other side. Slip each dipped patty into frying pan. Slowly brown each side. Turn several times if necessary.

Remove and serve hot with your favorite sauce. Try Seward Seafood Sauce. Serves two.

CHAPTER 5

EGGS HOW?

My first memories of the chicken fruit called eggs are somewhat vague. There were those mushed up things and the word *eggs* in the air. My mother was shoveling the things into my mouth. Often something distracted me. I've always assumed this was why she sometimes tried feeding my ear.

Mother's patience and the ever-present washcloth saved the day, as usual. In fact, the washcloth, back in the days before Easy-Wipes, Pop-Ups, and other modern mothers' delights were invented, became almost like the Teddy bear to a child. The newspaper cartoonist may draw security blankets, but in my far-distant youth I looked to the washcloth for security. Are our grandkids missing something? Their mothers aren't!

At eight I was throwing old hard-cooked eggs at the seagulls. Also at my friend Teddy, my usual partner in accidents. I can still remember the rotten hard-cooked egg I threw, he caught, and threw back at me. It hit me high on the forehead to the right of the eye. In my athletic twist to avoid the missile, or minimize the damage, I fell off the dock. Now, a good story would be how I caught the egg while in mid-fall to the water twelve feet below. In truth, I spent the time yelling loudly.

I went home soaked in sea water, and wouldn't you know, Mother met me at the door, washcloth in hand. She had feared much worse and was relieved that I had only fallen off the dock for the eleventh time.

In spite of doubtful egg memories I have been fond of the little darlings for as long as I can remember. I've written about the boat eggs of my youth. They were called boat eggs because they were delivered by steamship, not laid by boats. Way back in my youth the weekly steamship brought us everything in the way of food we didn't catch or shoot. The landlubbers referred to the great steamships as boats, a practice to shame any sailor. In fact, "Meeting the Boat" was usually the social event of the week.

Some dressed in their finest clothing for the occasion and others, like the ragamuffin kids, my friends and me, went looking like escapees from the slums. Everyone attended who could get away from whatever they were doing.

The dock would be full of people acting much like the present-day cocktail party guests, without the ever-present glass in hand. Not that there wasn't a bit of drinking going on. It was done from the bottle and around the corner of the warehouse, out of sight of the women.

The first thrill of the boat (ship) landing was throwing the lead line, a fist-sized, twine-wrapped ball of lead on the end of the long line. With it the heavy mooring lines were pulled ashore and, when the ship reached the right position, made fast to the dock. There was always the threat that the lead ball might hit one of the spectators, but they were a brave (or foolish) lot who stood their ground. Better to be hit than lose one's place in the group. Nor was there a mad stampede to catch the ball, as with fans at a baseball game, but rather a sudden compression of bodies to one or the other side of the perceived path of the ball and line.

Some lasting friendships began when young men and women came into such sudden contact. I did mention that it was a social event, didn't I? As at any social event, positioning was all-important.

On rare occasions a spectator was actually struck by this flying ball of lead, but I can remember only one. A young lady — shall we call her Cleo? — had been in town only a month. She had worked hard to establish herself in the community. She was most strict and proper in everything. As someone mentioned to Mother, "Butter wouldn't melt in her mouth!" Now, that's cool. It was generally assumed that she had her sights set on marriage into one of the town's leading families.

Came the day her still-new boss invited Cleo to "meet the boat." I'm sure it was her first step up the social ladder. The boat approached the dock, the young sailor in the bow twirling the lead line about his head. Some suggested that Cleo had caught his eye and he subconsciously threw the ball at her. I never believed that for a moment. The ball flew out over the crowd's heads and there was the usual surge as the people opened a space for the ball to land. The only one who failed to move was Cleo. We can assume that no one had explained the ground rules to her, and she was standing on ground zero.

At the last second her escort recognized her danger, grabbed her, and jerked her forward. No doubt he saved her life, as the ball, aimed for her head, struck her between the shoulder blades. She fell gracefully forward into her boss's arms, taking him down in what looked like a flying tackle. They hit the dock with her stretched out on top of him. He may have hit his head, as he made no move to get up.

People rushing to see whether she was hurt stopped cold at what happened next. Cleo raised her head and screamed, I suspect more in anger than in pain. Then she spewed forth about a dozen words which, in my youthful innocence, I had never heard from a woman. Her eyes then lost their glazed look, she realized what she had done, and she fainted.

Cleo left town shortly afterward, moved to the up-and-coming young city of Anchorage, married well and reared a big family, but never again did she meet a boat, train, or plane. I always thought of her as quite a woman, a real survivor. In fact, I liked her the first time I saw her. She smiled at me when I was ten years old.

Now that we have the weekly boat secured to the dock, let's get back to boat eggs. Shortly after delivery by the chickens, these eggs were refrigerated and in due time came their turn to be shipped to Alaska. You naturally ship the oldest eggs first, so you never can break out of the cycle. Extended storage gave boat eggs their distinctive flavor. You have to grow up with it or you wouldn't tolerate it. Fortunately, I did. Up to an age I refuse to discuss, I had never eaten a fresh egg. It had no taste at all.

Would you believe that, back then, we even tried to extend the life of the boat eggs by a method other than refrigeration? They were stacked carefully in a crock and covered with a sodium silicate solution we called water glass, which was supposed to seal out air and limit further changes in flavor. Yes, we had such a crock at our house. I just had a thought: could that have been where we got the word *crocked*?

I mentioned throwing rotten hard-cooked eggs at the gulls. Now you know where the eggs came from. By the time we got down to the two layers at the bottom of the crock, they were totally inedible. Even the gulls, which will eat anything, wouldn't touch them.

Today it's almost impossible to find a boat egg in Alaska. Most eggs are brought in by truck or plane, trucked to major marketing areas, and flown to the bush. It's been more than eight years since I was last offered a boat egg. It was out on Bristol Bay, where my host family's eggs were still coming to them by boat. I knew it the moment my hostess broke two eggs into her frying pan. My nose told me, and my stomach rejected the thought of them. I ate the hotcakes, reindeer sausage and toast, messed up the eggs, and "couldn't eat another bite."

Then, as I lifted the plate to hand it to my hostess, the smell triggered something far back in my mind and I had to try. I put the plate back down and took one bite. It was awful. I spit it back onto the plate.

"After reading your first book I thought you, of all people, could eat these eggs," my hostess said with a grin. "At least I had hopes. Should I feed them to the ravens?"

"Not if you like having ravens around," I told her.

From that day on it's been fresh eggs or none, and I keep searching for more and better ways to cook them. My doctor now limits my egg intake, which increases the incentive to make them different and better.

HOMETOWN BAKED EGGS

Here is a recipe you can claim came from your hometown. I know because the woman who gave it to me came from the west coast of France. She claimed it was from her hometown, which has a name I can neither spell nor pronounce. The taste was fine.

2 tablespoons butter (margarine
   if you have to)
4 slices Canadian bacon (ham is
   acceptable)
4 slices Swiss cheese
8 eggs
1/3 cup heavy cream
salt and pepper
1 teaspoon paprika

Use 4 small baking dishes, or ramekins, to bake and serve this dish.

Butter the interior of each baking dish. Lay a slice of bacon or ham on the bottom of each dish. Add a slice of Swiss cheese. Break 2 eggs into each dish. Divide cream among the dishes. Salt and pepper to taste.

Slide baking dishes into a preheated 350°F oven for approximately 6 minutes. The whites should be just set and the yolks still soft.

Remove from oven, sprinkle with paprika and serve right in the baking dish. Serves four.

MOTHER'S CURRIED EGGS

I remember one time an ill-advised young man asked my older brother whether this recipe was just a way to hide the taste of boat eggs. He was assured firmly that this was not the case at all! Mother said it was a recipe her mother had used back on the farm. For a city girl, that's a good story, too. I was young enough and smart enough to confine my activity to eating the results.

6 eggs
1/2 cup mayonnaise or white
    sauce
salt and pepper
1/4 cup all-purpose flour
1/2 teaspoon curry powder (more
    if you're into it)
1 cup bread crumbs
6 tablespoons vegetable oil

Hard-cook and chill 4 of the eggs. Peel and chop them fine. Add enough mayonnaise or white sauce to hold the eggs together. Salt and pepper to taste. Divide mixture into 4 equal-sized patties.

Combine flour and curry powder in a bowl.

Beat remaining 2 eggs. Dip each patty in flour, then into beaten egg and roll in bread crumbs. Chill in refrigerator for 30 minutes.

In a frying pan over medium heat, brown both sides of the patties in vegetable oil. Serve at once. Serves two to four.

ART'S
CREAMED EGGS

Art is a great creator of good things to eat, using anything that's available. He also has the best stocked cupboards, refrigerator, and deep freeze I have ever seen. When he cooks he tends to open every door in the kitchen and just grab from here and there. I love what he creates. Here's an example.

1 10 3/4-ounce can cream of
    chicken soup
1 10 3/4-ounce can cream of
    celery soup
1 cup whole milk
1 4-ounce can mushroom stems
    and pieces
1/4 teaspoon dill weed
1 teaspoon tarragon, crumbled
1 tablespoon cornstarch
1/2 tablespoon water
10 eggs, hard-cooked and
    chopped
1/4 cup white wine (sauterne if
    available)

Combine soup, milk, mushrooms, dill weed, and tarragon in a pan over medium heat. Mix well. Combine cornstarch with water and add to pan. Stir until mixture thickens. Add chopped eggs and stir. When heated, and just before serving, add the wine.

Art gave us a choice of fresh toasted bread, English muffins, or fresh biscuits under this delightful mixture. Once I served it over waffles fresh from the waffle iron. You might try it with frozen toaster waffles. It joins other foods willingly. Serves four.

EGGS ARTHUR

Yep! This is another of my friend Art's recipes. He made it first to impress his mother-in-law. His second wife's mother was smarter and enjoyed the dish. I know because I was there the night he served it to her as well as being best man at his wedding. And I stole the recipe.

6 eggs, beaten
1 cup whole milk
1 teaspoon salt
2 teaspoons sugar
1/2 cup Monterey Jack cheese, cut into 1/4-inch cubes
8 ounces cottage cheese
3 ounces cream cheese
3 tablespoons butter, softened
1/2 cup all-purpose flour
1 teaspoon baking powder

In a medium-sized bowl combine eggs, milk, salt, and sugar. Mix and add the cheeses and butter.

Grease a 9-by-12-inch casserole and pour this mixture into it. In another bowl combine flour and baking powder. Add flour to the casserole and mix well.

Slide casserole into a preheated 325°F oven. Bake for 40 minutes or until the mixture is set. Remove from oven, wait 5 minutes, and serve. Serves four to six.

NELSON SCRAMBLE

This is another recipe which dates back to the days when I caught and cooked seafood in large quantities. We usually had leftovers in the morning. It became a family tradition to have eggs scrambled with seafood.

3 tablespoons butter
1/2 cup minced onions
1/2 cup minced green pepper (or red pepper for color)
6 ounces seafood, fish, crab, shrimp, or a can of tuna, flaked
1 teaspoon lemon juice
1 teaspoon grated lemon peel (optional)
1 teaspoon dry parsley, finely crumbled
5 eggs, lightly beaten
salt and pepper

In a frying pan over medium heat melt butter and sauté onions and peppers. Add seafood, lemon juice and peel, parsley, and eggs. Salt and pepper to taste and quickly scramble the mixture until it's done to your liking. Serves four.

NOTE: If you are short of seafood, add a can of mushrooms to the mix. Or use your imagination to expand. . .

CLAM EGG CHINESE

One of the easiest egg dishes to cook is the ever-famous Egg Foo Young. I have no idea how long this recipe has been in our family, as I grew up with the taste in my mouth. We had an abundance of clams, in the front yard even, and you know we had boat eggs. The two were bound to come together.

5 eggs
1/2 teaspoon salt
1/8 teaspoon medium chili
    powder
1/2 cup minced onions
1 can bamboo shoots, chopped
1 4-ounce can mushroom pieces
    and stems
1 garlic clove, minced
1 can minced clams, drained (or
    fresh)
2 tablespoons soy sauce
4 tablespoons vegetable oil
1 teaspoon sesame oil

In a medium-sized bowl combine eggs, salt, and chili powder and beat lightly. Add onions, bamboo shoots, mushrooms, garlic, clams, and soy sauce. Mix well.

Heat oil in a wok or frying pan over medium heat. When oil is hot, drop 3/4-cup measures of the mixture into it. Cook each cupful as you would a pancake. Brown one side and turn over to brown the other side. Set the finished cake aside and go on to the next, until batter is used up.

Keep warm and serve all at once, or one at a time as they come out of the pan. Serves four.

Extra soy sauce or oyster sauce is nice to serve with the cakes. I've even used catsup, heaven forbid.

BAKED EGG SALAD

It was fortunate I tasted this salad before I heard the name. The name alone can put rather messy thoughts in the human mind. The salad on my plate was not only good but had a taste attractive in a different way.

vegetable oil spray
16 eggs
aluminum foil
1 cup mayonnaise
2 tablespoons minced onions
1 tablespoon minced celery
1 tablespoon dry parsley,
      crumbled (or freshly minced)
2 dashes pepper sauce (Tabasco)
salt and pepper
lettuce

Preheat oven to 350°F. Set out 2 9-inch pie pans. Spray with a shortening such as Pam.

Into each pan break 8 eggs. Cover pans with foil and slide into oven. Cook for 30 minutes, until eggs are set and appear hard-cooked. Remove, set on a rack to cool, and loosen edges of the eggs.

When cool turn the pie plates over on your cutting board, one at a time. With a sharp knife cut the cooked eggs into 1/4-inch squares and place in a medium-sized bowl.

Do the same to the second pan of eggs, and add to the bowl.

Add mayonnaise, onions, celery, parsley, and pepper sauce. Mix, adding salt and pepper to taste. Mix again and pack mixture into a ring mold. Chill for about 4 hours. Can be made the day before serving if you wish.

Turn out onto a lettuce-lined platter and slice to serve. Serves eight to ten.

NOTE: Sometime, change the pepper sauce to 2 teaspoons of curry powder for a different taste treat.

SEMI-GREEK SCRAMBLED EGGS

Someone sent me a jar of Greek olives just so I could try this recipe. I opened the jar, tasted the olives, and tossed them out the window. If you've never tried Greek olives, don't. The recipe sounded good so I made it, substituting ripe olives.

12 eggs
1/4 cup water
3/4 teaspoon dry oregano,
   crumbled
1/8 teaspoon black pepper
2 tablespoons butter
8 ounces feta or Jack cheese, cut
   in 1/2-inch chunks
1 2-ounce can ripe olives, minced
1 small, diced tomato
1 tablespoon dry, crumbled
   parsley

Combine eggs, water, oregano, and pepper in a bowl and mix with a fork.

Add butter to a frying pan over low heat and when it's melted and coating the pan, add egg liquid. As the eggs begin to set, shove set portions aside and allow still-liquid portions access to the heated pan surface. Cook until all eggs are softly set.

Sprinkle cheese chunks evenly over eggs. Slide the frying pan under the broiler for 1 or 2 minutes, until the cheese begins to soften.

Remove from heat, sprinkle olives, tomatoes, and parsley over surface of the dish. Cut into wedges and serve. Serves four to six.

CREAMY
BLUE EGGS

If the title hasn't discouraged you, you're in for a treat. I found these little jewels on a tray at a social gathering. I approached them with all the caution learned in sixty years in Alaska, yet the attitude of the experimenter. After my first one I moved back into the line, which was rapidly eliminating their presence.

I managed a second, and had to have the recipe. The cook was identified through my hard-earned investigative experience and I moved in for the grab. She proved to be a pushover and a fan of my first cookbook. I hope she approves of this offering.

6 eggs, hard-cooked and chilled
2 ounces plain cream cheese
3 tablespoons mayonnaise
2 tablespoons blue or Roquefort
    cheese
black pepper

Begin with chilled eggs. Peel and cut in half lengthwise. Remove yolks to a small bowl.

Soften cream cheese and mix with egg yolks. When well-mixed add the mayonnaise, blue cheese and pepper to taste.

Fill white halves of eggs with mixture. Arrange on a serving dish and chill again before serving. The way I calculate this treat, it serves two.

NOTE: I've been known to add minced ripe olives to the presentation, as well as minced onions, and for one occasion I added chopped red peppers, for a red, white, and blue effect.

QUICHE FOR FOUR

For years I had not been over-joyed with the idea of making quiche. I suspect the "real man doesn't eat quiche" bit had infected me. Not that I had any doubts, but — . Then one day I was placed in the position of being disagreeable or eating the stuff. It was a recipe I just knew I could improve upon, and I did. Try it!

1/2 cup chicken stock (chicken bouillon cubes and water an acceptable substitute)
1/2 cup chopped onions
4 eggs
2 cups whole milk
1/4 teaspoon ground nutmeg
1/4 teaspoon black pepper
1 tablespoon grated Parmesan cheese
1 4-ounce can sliced mushrooms, drained

Add stock to a small saucepan over medium heat and stir in onions. Cook for about 3 minutes or until onions are tender. Drain onions and reserve.

In a medium-sized bowl beat eggs lightly. Add milk, nutmeg, pepper, and cheese.

Divide onions and mushrooms evenly among 4 ramekins or baking dishes. Pour in the egg liquid again dividing equally.

Preheat oven to 350°F. Set the ramekins in a baking pan large enough to hold them and at least 2 inches deep. Pour water into pan around ramekins to within 1/2 inch of the ramekin tops. Slide into oven and bake for 25 minutes. Test with a knife. If it comes out clean, the quiche is done. Serve hot to four.

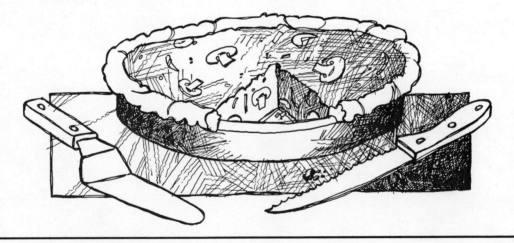

CHAPTER 6

SALAD CHOW

I am lucky to have grown up in Alaska. I've always known that. True, it was during the time we older folks remember as the Great Depression, but we had known hard times before the crash and our lifestyle changed little. During the fishing season there were jobs, even though the pay was minimal, for most people who wanted work. The usual pattern was for the entire family, right down to ten-year-old boys like me, to work hard during the season. Our family worked for the cannery. Dad and my older brother skippered cannery tenders, Mother worked on the cannery line, and I worked in the can loft. There were no child-labor laws then, and I was happy with the ten cents an hour I was paid. The four of us had one pot for the money and each put in whatever he earned. Ten hours gave me a whole dollar to add to the pot.

During those years we never went hungry, thanks to our earnings and nature's bounty. The forest provided birds, venison, and an occasional small animal for the cooking pot. The sea and its beaches provided clams, crabs, and several varieties of fish. The truth is, we often ate better than the wealthy do today. We were a happy people, and life was good.

Yes, some people who came to Alaska weren't so wonderful. We got our share of nonconformists, malcontents, and downright criminals. Fortunately they were easy to identify, so they didn't last long.

When an individual showed signs of being troublesome, the first step toward correction was ostracism. He became almost invisible. At this point, mending his ways could restore him to social acceptance.

If the individual didn't have the sense to understand ostracism, step two was necessary. He was asked to leave the community. If he went, fine. If not, step three was executed. That consisted of presenting the individual with a blue ticket to board the next steamer going in either direction. He was escorted to the dock and shown the gangplank. Usually he went up the gangplank under his own power, with "Don't come back!" ringing in his ears. If he didn't go, a fist was applied in the right place and he was carried aboard.

The criminal element was something else. In most communities there was a local marshal to tend to drunks and minor problems, and a U.S. deputy marshal passed through on occasion. He took the more serious offenders to wherever the district court was sitting. But all too often there wasn't enough evidence to convict the criminal and he returned to the community a free man, arrogant because he had beaten the criminal justice system.

For this reason the "Winchester Law" was acceptable if a person was protecting his life or his property. A dead body lying in such a position as to have been an obvious danger to the shooter was accepted as a normal death, if not a suicide. The fool should have known what to expect.

If a woman shot a man, the self-defense plea was almost always accepted — maybe not without a few sly comments about a "Winchester Divorce." I remember hearing Dad talk to one or another young man who was about to marry a widow. He always asked, "You do know how her former husband died?" Dad was a great people gardener. He liked to plant the seed of thought in the younger men. It would sometimes flourish into doubt.

Still another method of inflicting justice is seldom talked about now, and even less often when it was practiced. It was called the "Bottom Walk," and it might overtake the individual who was guilty of a major crime, such as murder, rape, or robbing fish traps. The latter was then the Alaskan equivalent to stealing a man's horse in the Old West. A sack of coal was tied to the feet of the culprit. Then he was taken out to deep water and instructed to walk ashore.

I can only hope that method was used with great restraint, as it is contrary to the American system of justice. One thing is for sure, however: the rate of recidivism was zero.

If all this makes Alaskans sound like an intolerant lot, let me assure you that we were not. We took great pride in the fact that Alaska was the land of the new leaf, the refuge of the individual who had made mistakes and wanted to turn his life around. It was considered very bad form to inquire into an individual's past. He was judged and accepted, or rejected, by how he conducted himself in the community.

Let's consider one of the good people of my community. Heading my list would be Helen Griffith. She and John lived on the hill above the ocean dock, and I doubt if there ever was a happier couple. The only flaw in their lives was the lack of children of their own, but they didn't complain. They reared twenty children of other people. It seemed that every time a steamer docked, it brought young people who ran eagerly up the hill. For many of them the Griffith home had been theirs too, yet many were first-time visitors who just wanted to meet Helen and John. Their fame as wonderful parents had spread.

As you can imagine, Helen lived by the steamer schedules. She always had pies baked to serve guests from the ship, and her pies seldom went begging. If the ship stayed for hours, loading or unloading, she would whip out a meal for her guests.

Mother and Helen were great friends, and I discovered early in my life that visits to Helen always meant food. I'll have to admit to checking Helen's windowsills for cooling pies, then running the half-mile home to suggest to Mother that we go visit Helen. I've never been sure whether Mother tumbled to my scheming. If she didn't, it was the only thing I ever put on her!

On several occasions the whole family went to Helen and John's to dinner. Males were allowed to pass through Helen's kitchen only if they were delivering groceries or carrying wood to the living-room heater. During her child-rearing years, Helen laid down strict rules. Girls had the run of the kitchen and the chores performed there were for girls. I didn't mind. The cookie jar sat in the middle of the dining-room table, available to anyone who might feel the need of a cookie fix.

You can imagine that Helen did not approve of my helping Mother when she opened her restaurant. Many times Helen came down to help Mother. She was skilled at turning out pastry and cookies, and she was a wonder with salads. I remember hearing her tell Mother, "I never served exactly the same salad twice in a month. Give them variety and you'll keep them coming."

Salads remind me of tuna, and tuna reminds me of another interesting character, "Tuna" Thompson, a fisherman who lived in Cordova in my youth. Tuna don't usually move that far north in the Pacific Ocean, so he didn't earn his nickname from fishing in these waters. He earned it with his mouth. It seemed he had worked on tuna clippers out of southern California. He claimed that was the only real way to make a living, and he was so loudmouthed about it that people began wondering aloud why he was fishing in Alaska. He didn't care to answer.

In fact, my older brother asked the question one night in a local saloon. Ken said liquor started the trouble, but I've always suspected that Tuna had other problems. He took a swing at Ken. Other men had made the same mistake, and it was considered near fatal.

Ken's return blow put Tuna down and should have ended the matter, but Tuna made a second mistake. He climbed back onto his feet, found a blurry outline he deduced to be Ken, and swung at it. In fact, he even staggered up and swung the third time.

Now, the unwritten rule of the waterfront was, if you put a man down, he's yours to take care of until he's on his feet again. Sort of like, you make a mess, you clean it up. So Ken left the saloon with Tuna over his shoulder, intending to take him back to his boat and toss him onto his bunk.

The tide was low, and getting Tuna aboard meant climbing ten or twelve feet down a ladder to where his craft was moored. Ken was halfway down when he detected signs that Tuna was coming to. The middle rung of a vertical ladder isn't the easiest place to renew a fight, so Ken just slid Tuna off his shoulder and let him fall into the water between his ship and the dock piling.

Now Ken had a new problem, getting the half-conscious man up the side of the ship. Ken tossed Tuna a line and began to pull. Halfway up, he stopped pulling, looked down into the miserable face, and asked, "Who hung the name 'Tuna' onto you, and why?" The answer was unprintable. Ken dropped Tuna back into the sea. When his head surfaced again, Ken asked, "Who and why?"

Tuna was ready to talk. His story went something like this:

"I was working aboard the *Rose II* out of San Pedro. After a run of bad luck the skipper reduced me from fisherman to cook. By the second day I was beginning to enjoy the job. I whipped out a fine big salad, and for a final touch I opened two cans of tuna and mixed it into the salad.

"The skipper took one mouthful, then sprayed it across the galley and yelled 'TUNA!' at the top of his voice. I spent the next week in the lifeboat, and I've been Tuna ever since."

"Why use the name up here?" Ken asked.

"I couldn't get away from it. The way fishermen wander around, someone was sure to know me. And now I suppose you'll tell everyone. Right?"

Ken didn't. Even I didn't hear the story until Tuna was long gone. As Ken explained it, "Kid, after you've saved a man's life, you have a proprietary interest in his person. I found myself having to protect Tuna from the story of his past. He was my private nut, I guess."

Years later I heard another story about how Tuna got his name. According to that one, he was caught stealing canned tuna from an employer. So Tuna, too, was a storyteller. Take your choice.

Don't let one man's tale of troubles with fish in a salad keep you from adding seafood to yours. As far as I'm concerned, there's very little that cannot be added successfully to a salad, and seafoods have always been among my favorites. What would you expect from a guy with webs between his fingers? Years in salt water will do it, you know.

KING KRAB
SUMMER SALAD

One of the scientific wonders of modern times is the artificial crab meat called King Krab. As greedy king crab fishermen, ill-advised fishery management, and willing processors have almost destroyed the king crab natural stocks by over-fishing, we still have something tasty to add to salads. It is well worth trying.

2 cucumbers, peeled and thinly
    sliced
1 mild onion, sliced and separated
    into rings
1 cup packaged croutons or diced
    toast
1/2 cup mayonnaise
1/3 cup cider vinegar
1/2 teaspoon ground paprika
salt and pepper
1/2 pound King Krab, sticks or
    bulk pack cut in chunks
1 head lettuce
1 avocado, peeled and thinly sliced

In a large mixing bowl combine cucumbers, onion rings, and croutons.

In a smaller bowl combine mayonnaise, vinegar, and paprika. Mix well. Salt and pepper to taste.

Add salad dressing to the large bowl and mix well. Then add Krab pieces.

Line your serving bowl with lettuce leaves and turn Krab mixture carefully into it. Try not to break up Krab chunks. Top salad with avocado slices as a garnish.

Serves two to four.

NOTE: King Krab is the official trade name for artificial crab. This salad can be made with real crab, too. It's even excellent with cold cooked halibut chunks.

MATANUSKA FREEZER SLAW

Alaska's Matanuska Valley is famous for its huge cabbages. There is little you can do with an eighty-pound cabbage, except show it off in the Alaska State Fair. But those little twenty-pounders can be put to good use. This is one way people put down the makings of a winter coleslaw in the freezer. I suggest you try a small recipe the first time, like this:

1 cabbage head, three to four
    pounds, shredded
1 teaspoon salt
2 large carrots, shredded
1 green pepper, finely chopped
1/2 cup sugar
1 teaspoon celery salt
1 tablespoon mustard seed
1 cup vinegar
1/4 cup water

Spread out cabbage in a large bowl. Sprinkle on salt and allow to stand for an hour. Add carrots and green pepper.

In a pan over medium heat combine remaining ingredients. Bring to a boil and wait 1 minute. Then pour over vegetables. Mix well.

Allow to cool. Estimate the amount you will need to thaw and serve for a single meal and package in freezer bags. Store in the freezer until needed.

Remove from the freezer at least an hour before the salad will be needed. Empty into a serving bowl and serve.

NOTE: This already dressed salad is fine, but I've been known to add a glob of mayonnaise and stir it in just before serving.

LILLIAN'S HOT POTATO SALAD

My sister-in-law, Lillian, was the first to serve me hot potato salad. It was on my first visit to Ken and his new bride. She was from a German family of excellent cooks. When she discovered my interest in cooking, she often slipped me good recipes. She would have been happy to share this one with you, I know.

9 medium-sized potatoes
1 pound bulk-pack pork sausage
1 large onion, chopped
1 1/2 cups beef stock (bouillon and
    water okay)
2/3 cup red wine vinegar
1 cup thinly sliced celery
1 teaspoon salt
1/4 teaspoon black pepper
2 eggs, hard-cooked
1/3 cup sliced ripe olives
    (2-ounce can)

In a large saucepan over medium heat, with just enough water to cover, cook potatoes about 20 minutes or until tender. Drain and cool potatoes and dice into a large bowl.

In a large frying pan over medium heat, cook sausage, breaking it up into small pieces in the process. When it's browned, drain half the fat. Add onion to the pan and cook another 10 minutes.

Add beef stock and vinegar and simmer another 5 minutes. Add celery, potatoes, salt and pepper and stir until well-mixed and heated. Turn out into a shallow serving dish. Garnish with chopped eggs and olives. Serves six to eight as a meal unto itself.

SOUR-CREAMED CUCUMBERS

Since I have sold enough books to be independently wealthy (a dream, not a fact!), I now have a small greenhouse attached to the back of the garage. It is one of my greatest joys during the days of long light in summer. The tomatoes, cukes, and other delights make summer a time of rejoicing. I always seem to have a surplus of cucumbers, even after handing them to family and neighbors with some abandon. They don't keep forever, so we have to dream up ways of eating the tasty delights. Here's a favorite recipe.

1 cucumber, European-style
*   (or 3 regular)*
1 teaspoon salt
1 cup sour cream
2 green onions, thinly sliced (tops
*   included)*
1 1/2 teaspoons snipped fresh dill
*   (or 1/2 teaspoon dill seed)*
1 tablespoon capers, drained
*   (optional)*
1/4 teaspoon black pepper
1 tablespoon sugar

On your cutting board slice cucumber into thin slices. Spread out slices and sprinkle with salt. Slide into a bowl and refrigerate for 1 hour.

Remove from refrigerator and drain liquid from the bowl. Add sour cream and toss carefully. Add onions, dill, capers, pepper, and sugar. Toss again. Cover and return to refrigerator until ready to serve. Serves two to four.

SUPER
SWEET 'n' SOUR
SALAD

The main crop of our Matanuska garden is potatoes, but a close second is broccoli. It does extremely well here, as do most cabbage family plants. My aim each fall is to have a hundred packages of broccoli in the freezer. With all the other delights in the freezer we usually find twenty packages still left in the spring. They have to be used before the new crop of broccoli appears. With this recipe you'd think it was fresh. Almost?

4 bacon slices
1/2 cup cider vinegar
1/2 cup water
2 teaspoons sugar
salt and pepper
2 packages broccoli, thawed
    frozen, chopped, and drained
1 medium onion, peeled, sliced,
    and separated into rings

In your large frying pan over medium heat, cook bacon until crisp. Remove slices, drain, and crumble.

Retain only 4 tablespoons of bacon grease in the pan. Add vinegar, water, sugar, and salt and pepper to taste. Bring liquid to a boil.

Combine broccoli and onions in a serving bowl. Pour on the boiling liquid and toss until broccoli is well-coated with liquid. Sprinkle bacon bits over the top and serve. Serves four.

WIGGLER'S GREEN PIZZA

Back in the days when I thought property management in the City of Anchorage was a good retirement business, I met some interesting people. One day there came this woman of undetermined age but with an extremely well-cared-for body, looking for an apartment. When asked what she did for a living she stated, "Wiggle!" Yes, she was a dancer, and an excellent cook. She was studying to work at the latter profession when "wiggling" was no longer a viable career. She had some interesting ideas, about cooking, I mean. Like this one.

2 heads lettuce
1/2 pound sausage, hard type, salami, pepperoni, reindeer, or whatever
3 tomatoes, sliced
8 ounces Mozzarella cheese, shredded
1 4-ounce can sliced mushrooms
1 4-ounce can sliced olives
1 green pepper, cored and sliced
1 8-ounce can tomato sauce
3 tablespoons minced onions
1 tablespoon red wine vinegar
1 teaspoon Italian seasoning
salt and pepper (also cayenne if wanted)

Separate the lettuce carefully and lay a double layer on a 10- to 12-inch serving plate. This will act as the pizza crust.

Over the lettuce spread a layer of thinly sliced sausage, topped with tomato slices. Add a layer of cheese and then mushrooms, olives, and green pepper slices.

In a bowl combine tomato sauce, onions, vinegar, Italian seasoning, and salt and pepper to taste (add cayenne here if you dare).

When serving time approaches, drizzle some of the dressing around the pizza, but save most for individuals to dress their separate dishes of salad pizza. Serves four.

WAYBACK JAPANESE CARROT SALAD

I first tasted this salad or something very similar when I was about nine years old. My best friend was a Japanese boy next door. Teddy and I were inseparable for a couple of years, fifty-odd years ago. We had dinner at each other's homes on many occasions. My first taste of this salad several years ago brought back those good memories. I sneak it into our meals every once in a while, just for effect.

1 1/2 cups peeled and finely
    shredded carrots
1 cup peeled and finely shredded
    turnips
vinegar, sugar, and lettuce

Combine shredded carrots and turnips in a bowl. Add vinegar and sugar to your taste and water to cover vegetables. Let stand in a refrigerator for an hour.

Drain well and turn out onto a lettuce-lined plate. Serves two to four. A garnish of other fresh vegetables around the salad is appropriate. Our favorite is raw sugar snap pea pods.

NOTE: If the somewhat vague dressing instructions bother you, try the Summer Sweet 'n' Sour Salad Dressing on page 193.

ONCE-A-YEAR SALAD

The name of this salad is not so realistic as it was back when fruit came to Alaska in limited quantities and only at certain times of year. Did I mention expensive? It was, and such a salad as this for our large family was really a once-a-year event. We had to be sure everyone would be home for the occasion so no one would feel left out. Now we seem to have it any time we wish. Even the melon is available in the freezers.

1 large melon, cantaloupe or
    honeydew
4 navel oranges
4 bananas
1 8-ounce package pitted dates
1 cup sour cream
1/3 cup pineapple juice
1/3 cup mayonnaise

All fruit should be chilled before you begin. Peel, seed, and chunk melon. Peel and separate orange slices after removing as much white membrane as possible. Peel and slice bananas. Arrange the fruit in a flat serving bowl. Cut dates in quarters and sprinkle over the fruit.

GRANDMA'S MARSHMALLOW SALAD

It's nice to realize we moderns have no lock on innovation. This grandma four generations back had recipes which certainly proved her originality. In fact, there is nothing like reading old family recipe collections to bring us closer to the past. Even when they use such measurements as "half an egg shell," you know it's much like one tablespoonful today. I have to admit that some ingredients have vanished from the stores and substitutions are necessary. Not for this recipe, though.

2 cups miniature marshmallows,
*   finely cut*
1 cup finely chopped walnuts
1 cup diced apples
1/2 cup whipped cream
*   (or Cool Whip)*
1 teaspoon sugar

In a bowl mix marshmallows, nuts, and apples together.

In a second bowl whip cream until stiff and blend in sugar. Pour whipped cream over the other mixture, stir and serve. Serves four.

NOTE: Penciled under Grandma's recipe, but who knows by whom in the line of those who had the book, "Try some of the new sliced pineapple cut in chunks."

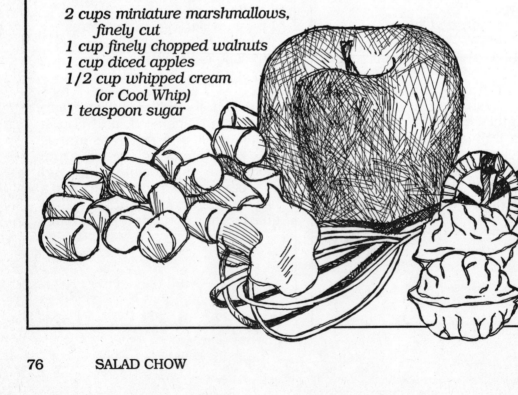

HOT BORSCHT SALAD

I first tasted this dish in Kodiak many years ago, but was unable to get the recipe as the Trooper was needed elsewhere. It was a taste that haunted me over the years. Then in the mail from one of you out there came a recipe that sounded hopeful. It wasn't the right one, but it did something else, sent me researching for the right recipe. This is my interpretation of all the ideas I found. Try it!

5 bacon slices
2 tablespoons butter or margarine
1 large onion, chopped
4 potatoes, boiled, then peeled and
    diced in 1/4-inch cubes
1 15-ounce can beets, diced (save
    the liquid)
3 tablespoons cider vinegar
salt and pepper

In a large frying pan over medium heat fry bacon until it's crisp. Remove and drain on paper toweling. Add butter to the pan.

Sauté onion for 5 minutes while stirring. Add potatoes and diced beets to the pan and heat for 2 minutes. Combine vinegar and 2 tablespoons of beet juice and add to pan. Stir to coat and color with beet juice. Salt and pepper to taste.

Turn out into a salad serving bowl and sprinkle with crumbled bacon. Serves four nicely.

NOTE: One recipe suggested mashing the ingredients just before adding the bacon. I didn't like the looks of the results, so I give you lumpy borscht salad.

REVOLUTION SALAD SEASONING

Every time I wander down the grocery aisles to the seasoning section, I marvel at the prices demanded for those small shaker jars of seasoning. They seem to go up in price weekly. Are you people actually buying the stuff? It's revolting. So I revolted and designed my own all-purpose salad seasoning. I like it better and mentally thumb my nose at the people who brought about the revolution. You, too, can fight back. Try this one!

5 tablespoons onion powder (bought in bulk store bins)
5 teaspoons garlic powder
5 teaspoons paprika
1/2 teaspoon coarsely ground black pepper (grind your own)
1 teaspoon celery seed
2 teaspoons poppy seed
1/2 cup toasted sesame seed
1 teaspoon salt (optional)

Combine all the ingredients and mix thoroughly. Fill your last empty "store-bought" shaker and store the remainder in a Zip-lock bag.

You can add the mixture to any salad dressing you whip up. Or use it for a sprinkle over salads. It's great over other foods as well — vegetables, fruit salads, cottage cheese, and anything needing a dash of color or taste.

NOTE: I usually mix a large batch with the same ratio of ingredients and divide and mix into shakers or bags, each with another ingredient, such as oregano, basil, marjoram, rosemary, sage, or thyme. I recommend some experimenting with seafood, chicken, and vegetables. You know, a dash of this or that. Who knows, you might get lucky, hit a combination you can package and sell, thereby joining the people on the other side of the revolution. Those making money!

CHAPTER 7

VEGETABLES WOW!

We who have lived all our lives in Alaska may look at vegetables in a different light from those Outside. No, I'm not referring to the "Northern Lights," or the longer, subdued light of winter. Winter is nearly all dark, mostly like the inside of a good root cellar. It used to be we went to the cellar and felt around by the light of a lantern for some vegetable that had survived the last cold snap. No longer. I have a huge freezer, and every vegetable I grow that will stand freezing is stored there. Row after row of plastic bags in meal-sized amounts fill half the freezer. Only my potatoes are stored in bins in the garage. We hold this area at about forty degrees.

Our crop is heavy with peas, regular and sugar snap, and broccoli, although zucchini, carrots, brussels sprouts, turnips, rutabagas, and green beans occupy some space. So you see, we go

into every winter with a lot of good eating tucked away. This is today. How about in the past?

In my youth we lived in the coastal areas and seldom do you see gardens there. Heavy rainfall, cloudy weather, and a shortage of good soil long ago discouraged gardeners.

Even in the hard times we had to buy most of the vegetables that graced our table. Mainly they were the cheapest, such as potatoes, cabbage, and carrots. The huge Hubbard was the only member of the squash family we ever saw. All other vegetables were bought canned. I didn't know what asparagus was until after I was ten.

To balance this shortage, we had things on our table regularly — fish, clams, crab, and venison — that those in the Lower Forty-Eight seldom saw on theirs. We sure didn't starve.

It was people living in the isolated communities and camps in the Interior who suffered from the lack of vegetables to go with their moose and caribou. Some found themselves making salads from the inner bark of the "what-not tree." I still don't know which tree that was. I have heard that the loners in the Bush tried to blame the beaver for all the trees they killed. The beaver is partial to tree bark. I'm not, although I'll admit to tasting some in my search for the secret tree.

Of course we all know moose feed on the bark of select trees and bushes in their range. They are often seen nibbling on small bushes and trees, such as the tender crabapple tree in my backyard. A big moose, maybe even Hibrow Cow, ate it right down to the nubbin.

The nature of their feeding was duly noted by many early pioneers, as was the fact that the stomach of a freshly killed moose is full of partially digested salad. The Native people have been known to feed on this. I wonder who else. Enough on this subject before I lose all my readers. Hello! Is anyone still out there?

At one time I had a lot of people in the Bush depending upon me for their vegetables. I was working for a time as the grocery department shipping clerk for the old N.C. (Northern Commercial) Company in Anchorage. They were operating a charge-groceries system so the people in the Bush could leave standing orders to be sent to them each week. I had a card file listing the people and their likes and dislikes. No one wants to pay top prices and air freight on anything they don't want or can't eat.

After I had been there for a while, I had the letters "WSLB" in the corners of most cards. They trusted me to send them "what stuff looks best." Most had a limited dollar amount but some didn't care, they missed their vegetables that much.

The merchandise was selected with care and packed carefully for travel by air and in the cold. Our delivery man took it to the airplane so it didn't sit around in someone's warehouse and miss a plane. The pilot took the orders out to the villages. The recipients usually knew when he was coming and met the plane. It was an event in the weekly schedule. A grocery box left to sit unattended and freeze could ruin anybody's week.

There were a few of the standing order cards with "AB" in the other corner, which meant the weekly grocery box would be kicked out of the low-flying plane and delivered "airborne." These boxes got special packing, to the point we sometimes delivered eggs in the AB packages. It was a challenge and we didn't know until spring whether the eggs arrived all right.

In fact, near Christmastime, some bottles of Christmas spirit were brought to me for drop-packing. I had one rule: the bottle was packed in an oilskin bag. The bottle might break but one could drink or pour from a bag if necessary.

Parachutes? Are you kidding? I didn't know what they were until my best friend came home from the war as a paratrooper. For us it was snow piles, the pilot's good eye, and a free fall for the packages.

This reminds me of another story. (What doesn't?) Back in the 1930s my brother was part of a survey team that went in to survey one of the boundaries of Denali National Park, then known as Mount McKinley National Park. Surveying was done in the winter, when traveling was actually easier. A local Bush pilot was contracted to keep them supplied during the job. He landed on skis on a nearby lake, if there was one.

After one mission, the surveyors discovered that a critical commodity was missing from the order. Chris, the pilot, agreed to swing wide on one of his next flights and air-drop the missing merchandise. At this point in his story, my brother always mentions an evil gleam in the pilot's eye.

Two days passed. The crew was working in a low stand of birch. Suddenly Chris's plane came in on a strafing run and two items dropped from the pilot's side window. They looked about the size of cans of peaches. The crew dived for cover. One of the items struck the slowest man's head. Good bombing! Ken caught it as it bounced. He didn't see who got the other one.

For the next ten minutes Chris flew back and forth over the crew, air-dropping the necessary commodity one roll at a time but removing the wrappers before he dropped the rolls. They unrolled nicely as they fell. When the bombardment was over, he zoomed away with a friendly wiggle of his wings, and no doubt an evil gleam in his eye, leaving white streamers on a quarter of a mile of birch trees. Ken always ends this story with, "I had my roll. The rest of the guys spent two hours unwrapping the trees and rolling up the toilet tissue."

After the war, I was discharged from the Army and returned from overseas, which in my case meant crossing Ship Creek to Anchorage. I went to work for a wholesale company. Endless carload lots of vegetables and canned goods rolled across our docks. My still young and healthy muscles were taxed no end, unloading railroad cars. Then came the day a carload of onions appeared beside our warehouse. It had gone to Fairbanks and back, I think, and had spent several cold winter days on the way. Even before the car door was opened I knew something was wrong. Instead of the sharp, mouth-watering onion smell, I detected the repulsive smell of soggy onions. This carload of onions was garbage. I closed the door and went to the office to get the claim against the rail-road started.

Alas, I reported the problem to the boss, and promptly lost control. I was instructed to sort the good onions from the bad onions. Unless you've been involved in the same exercise, you have no idea how bad it was. For three days, my crew and I sorted onions every minute we could spare from our other duties. Gradually the ratio of good to bad onions diminished, until they were all bad.

Naturally, the news (or the smell) of our enterprise drifted uptown, and the company couldn't sell an onion anywhere. The sorting ended, but the problem didn't. Our stack of good onions in the warehouse was rapidly going gooey. The whole warehouse smelled of soggy onions, and so did most of the merchandise we were delivering. It was worse than an exercise in futility. It set the business back about a year in customer relations, and all because of one boss who didn't know when to cut his losses.

After this experience, you might think I would be down on onions. I'm not. I add them to anything an onion might improve, and I've even been known to serve sliced onions cooked in butter as the only vegetable with a dinner. Let's get on with some recipes.

GREAT GRANDMA'S CORN OYSTERS

Finding this recipe in Connie's grandmother's recipe collection was like finding gold to me. Having grown up in a land in which you can't grow real corn crops, the idea of having enough corn on the cob to make this dish is fantastic.

6 ears of corn
1 egg, beaten
1 teaspoon salt
1/2 teaspoon pepper
cracker crumbs
shortening

Grate corn ears slightly to break the skin of the kernels. With a dull knife, scrape all the pulp into a bowl. Add egg, salt and pepper and mix well.

Add enough cracker crumbs that you can shape mixture into oyster-sized balls. Place balls in a hot, well-greased frying pan. Flatten to half their height. Brown on one side, turn and brown the other side.

Remove to a warm plate until all the mixture is used. Serves two to four.

SERBIAN CABBAGE

My wife says I become a cabbage pusher during the fall. I can't seem to help planting too many cabbage plants and I hate to rototill the surplus under. You can eat only so much cole slaw and corned beef and cabbage during a summer, and there are all the other delightful vegetables growing around the cabbage. I want to eat them fresh, too. My cabbage-pushing reputation caused this recipe to turn up in my mail. This is just how I received it, word for word.

1 4-pound head of cabbage,
 finely shredded
1 13-ounce can evaporated milk
1 cup dry bread crumbs
1 teaspoon ground paprika
1 4-ounce cube butter

Preheat your oven to 350°F. While it's heating, search for your 4-quart casserole.

Pack cabbage shreds into casserole. Add can of milk.

Combine bread crumbs and paprika, mix well and sprinkle over cabbage. Dot with butter.

Bake in the oven for 30 minutes, covered. Remove cover and give dish another 30 minutes, or even longer to brown the bread crumbs.

Serve in casserole or turn out on a platter and surround with ham, or even corned beef. Serves four.

NOTE: I found no reason to change a thing in the recipe. It's obviously tried and true.

MATANUSKA PICKLED CARROTS

Another vegetable that grows well in this Matanuska Valley is the carrot. Naturally, after you have served them boiled, stewed, sliced, and grated, and added them to every dish you make, there will be some left. I had all I needed in the freezer and still had carrots left in the garden. Any suggestion would have been considered. Into this void of ideas came this recipe from a friend:

3 tablespoons vegetable oil
1 teaspoon salt
1 1/4 teaspoons sugar
2 cups peeled or scraped and
    shredded carrots
1 cup very thinly sliced green
    peppers
1/3 cup finely chopped celery
1/4 cup water
1 cup finely chopped onions
1/4 cup tomato catsup
2 tablespoons lemon juice

In a saucepan over medium heat combine 2 tablespoons oil, 1 teaspoon salt, and 1 teaspoon sugar. Add carrots, green peppers, celery, and water. Bring to a boil, reduce heat and simmer uncovered. Stir occasionally during the 5 to 10 minutes necessary for vegetables to become tender. Remove from heat.

In a second saucepan, sauté onions in 1 tablespoon oil and 1/4 teaspoon sugar until transparent. Add onions to carrot mixture and mix well. Add catsup and lemon juice and mix one more time.

Transfer carrots to a covered bowl and chill in the refrigerator. Serve cold as a salad, or as a garnish for fish dishes, or add some to your favorite sandwich. And finish the bowl as a midnight snack. Serves four as a salad.

NOTE: This dish is reported to keep for a week, but in my experience it is gone within two days.

MS. WATTS'S LENTIL SUPREME

The woman who offered me this recipe wished to remain unknown, but would accept Watts as an alias as long as I preceded it with Ms. She was blonde, with blue eyes and much more. The Tired Wolf had a momentary flash of rejuvenation, which faded all too fast. When she was gone I managed to read the recipe. I had to try it. I hope you will, too.

1/4 teaspoon cayenne
1 teaspoon paprika
1/2 teaspoon ground ginger
1/2 teaspoon ground cardamom
1/4 teaspoon garlic powder
1/4 teaspoon salt
1/8 teaspoon ground coriander
1/8 teaspoon ground cinnamon
2 teaspoons white vinegar
2 tablespoons water
2 large onions, chopped
1/4 cup vegetable oil
1/3 cup tomato paste
5 1/2 cups water
2 cups lentils
2 limes, cut in wedges (lemons
    okay)

In a small bowl combine cayenne, paprika, ginger, cardamom, garlic powder, salt, coriander, cinnamon, vinegar, and 2 tablespoons water. Mix into a smooth paste and set aside.

In a 5-quart pan over medium heat, sauté onions in oil for about 5 minutes. Stir in tomato paste and spice-bowl contents. Add 1/2 cup of water and cook for another 5 minutes, stirring.

Add remaining 5 cups of water and lentils. Bring mixture to a boil and reduce heat to simmer. Cook, covered, for 45 minutes, occasionally stirring. Test lentils. They should be soft to the bite. Add cooking time only if needed, and in small amounts.

Serve in bowls while still hot. Place slices of lime or lemon beside each bowl. Serves six to eight.

NOTE: Leftovers can be reheated. Like so many dishes, this seems to improve with time to mature.

CHARLIE'S COUSIN'S PATTIES

In my earlier cookbooks, I referred to the Chinese cook named Charlie, whom I knew in my childhood. Some fifty years after I last saw Charlie I received a letter from a young woman who was sure she was a cousin of Charlie's many times removed. I wouldn't doubt her for a minute. She seemed a nice young woman, she was a fan of my books, and she sent me a good recipe. What more proof does a man need?

1 1/2 cups pinto beans, cooked
(other varieties okay)
2 garlic cloves, minced
1/4 cup chopped green onions
1/4 cup finely chopped parsley
1 tablespoon lemon juice
1 teaspoon ground cumin
1/4 teaspoon crumbled basil
1/4 teaspoon crumbled thyme
1/4 teaspoon crumbled marjoram
1 egg, beaten
1 slice whole wheat bread,
crumbled
salt and pepper
Tabasco sauce
1/3 cup sesame seeds (or finely
chopped nuts)
4 tablespoons vegetable oil

In a flat-bottomed dish mash beans. Add garlic, onions, parsley, lemon juice, cumin, basil, thyme, marjoram, egg, and bread crumbs. Mix to blend. Salt and pepper to taste. Add dash or two of Tabasco if you like things hot.

Spread sesame seeds or nuts on a piece of wax paper. Drop a heaping tablespoonful of bean mixture onto the seeds. When both sides are coated, shape beans into patties about 2 1/2 inches across.

In a frying pan over medium heat add the oil. Brown the patties on both sides, about 1 1/2 minutes each side. Keep finished patties warm until serving time.

Serve two to four people who I'm sure would appreciate one of your favorite sauces. Maybe Mary's Yogurt-Mint Sauce on page 163.

INDIANA PARMESAN POTATOES

This recipe came from the cookbook of my wife's grandmother, twice-removed. Connie knows they passed through Indiana when they came out the Oregon Trail, way back when it took wagons and draft animals to make the trip. One can't but wonder what incident led to the naming of this dish. Were they glad to get there, or glad to leave? Maybe they just found some good potatoes.

6 medium-sized potatoes, peeled
*   and boiled*
1/4 teaspoon salt
1/8 teaspoon pepper
cayenne
1/4 pound butter
1 cup grated Parmesan cheese
*   (or any hard cheese)*

Slice potatoes 1/8-inch thick and arrange in a shallow baking pan, two or three slices high. Sprinkle salt, pepper, and (lightly) cayenne between layers. Dot with butter until it's gone. Sprinkle cheese over the top.

Slide into a hot oven until cheese is melted and browned. Serves four.

NOTE: A simple recipe that has stood the test of time. It's as tasty today as when Grandma jotted it into her cookbook more than a hundred years ago. Trying it is a form of time travel.

FRENCH POTATO PIE

There is a story drifting around that this is the first French potato dish to come to America. My grandmother came right out of Nova Scotia. She was of the third generation of a French migration to the land in the 1700s, when it was called Acadia. French fries seem to have gone the other way, into France from America. This is Grandma's recipe, adapted to the pastry mix available in a modern grocery store. Making your own crust is still acceptable.

1 package pie pastry mix, enough
    for two crusts
6 large potatoes, boiled and riced
1 cup cream, or whole milk
2 tablespoons butter
1 medium onion, sliced and
    sautéed to golden
salt and pepper
nutmeg

Line bottom and sides of a deep pie dish with pastry. Combine riced potatoes, cream, butter, and onion. Salt and pepper to taste. Fill pie shell with mixture and sprinkle top with nutmeg. Add top crust, crimp edges, and make several slits in top.

Slip into a preheated 350°F oven and bake until hot all the way through and the crust is brown. Check at 15 minutes and add time as necessary.

Remove and serve hot. Serves four.

NOTE: If you don't have a ricer, you should. It's a simple device that can improve the taste and texture of potatoes. Okay! Borrow a neighbor's to make this dish.

MRS. NELSON'S SPECIAL COMBO

This Nelson is not related to me, but then the Nelsons are only slightly fewer than the Johnsons and trying harder. She was a reader of my cookbooks and she wanted to contribute to my next one. I love fan letters, and good recipes. It is sad that so seldom do the two come in the same envelope. This time we had a Bingo!

6 beets, cooked, peeled, sliced, and chilled
3 potatoes, cooked, peeled, cubed, and chilled
3 dill pickles, chopped
2 cups garbanzo beans
2 medium onions, peeled and thinly sliced
salt and pepper
4 tablespoons cider vinegar
3 tablespoons salad oil (olive recommended)
1/4 cup dry red wine

In a large bowl combine beets, potatoes, pickles, garbanzos, and onions. Sprinkle with salt and pepper.

In a smaller bowl combine vinegar, oil, and wine. Whisk well and pour over vegetables. Toss to coat everything. Adjust seasoning if necessary. Serves six to eight as a nice hot-weather meal.

NOTE: In the land of the tin can, I made this using canned sliced beets, well-drained, and canned garbanzo beans/peas. It turned out just fine.

KIELBASA CABBAGE

When Al told me, "Come over to my house for dinner and bring a six-pack!" I assumed I would be drinking beer with dinner. I was one-third right. Two cans of the beer went into the cooking, two into Al and two into me. I sipped my first can as I took notes of his dinner preparations. I made only one minor change in his recipe.

2 12-ounce cans of beer, your choice
2 12-ounce packages Polish sausage, fully cooked
1 4-pound head green cabbage, coarsely chopped
1/4 head purple cabbage (1 pound), coarsely chopped
1 teaspoon sugar
1 teaspoon salt
1 tablespoon medium-hot chili powder

Pour 2 cans of beer into a 6-quart Dutch oven. Place it over medium heat and add sausage. Add extra water to cover them, if necessary. Reduce heat and simmer for 8 to 10 minutes to add the beer flavor. Do not boil sausages. Remove sausages and set aside. Keep warm.

Add cabbage, sugar, salt and chili powder to Dutch oven and mix well. Cover and simmer for 5 minutes. Check for tenderness. Add extra time if necessary. At the last moment before the cabbage is done, put sausage back on top to reheat.

Remove sausage, drain cabbage Save juice to drink if you absolutely can't waste the beer. Pile drained cabbage on a platter and top with sausage. Serves four to maybe six in a pinch.

NOTE: I've made the same recipe using other sausages and found it equally good. My change — no purple cabbage.

EDNA'S SWEET 'n' SOUR BAKED BEANS

It seems that none of my cookbooks get by without a baked bean recipe. I reviewed my four best recipes for baked beans, and three were already in books. I finally settled on Edna's recipe. She has been a willing contributor. I wondered how I missed it during the other selection processes. It's a large recipe and I've used it successfully at several potlatches, or potluck gatherings. I've always taken home an empty pan.

2 15-ounce cans lima or butter beans
1 15-ounce can green baby limas
1 15-ounce can red kidney beans
1 15-ounce can Boston baked beans
1 15-ounce can garbanzos
8 bacon slices
4 onions, peeled and sliced
1/2 cup brown sugar
1 teaspoon garlic powder
1 teaspoon salt
1 teaspoon dry mustard
1/2 cup cider vinegar
1 cup water

In your largest bowl empty the drained 6 cans of beans and set aside.

In a large frying pan over medium heat, fry bacon crisp. Remove bacon and drain. In bacon grease, sauté onions until they are tender.

Drain all but 2 tablespoons of bacon grease and add sugar, garlic powder, salt, mustard and vinegar to the pan. Add cup of water and simmer for 10 minutes.

Add frying-pan contents to beans, as well as crumbled bacon. Mix well and pour into a deep baking dish. Slide into 350°F preheated oven for 30 to 40 minutes.

Remove and keep warm until serving. Serves up to sixteen.

OLD-TIME SARATOGA CHIPS

From my researching into old cookbooks, it is obvious that people have been producing potato chips far longer than I had imagined. They had different names for the crisp delights. This recipe is out of a hundred-year-old cookbook. It's a simple one and I thought you might enjoy it.

potatoes (the amount you wish to process)
fat (animal renderings)
salt

Wash and peel the potatoes. Slice them extremely thin into a bowl of cold water. Let stand in water for an hour. Drain water and replace with fresh water. Soak for another 30 minutes. Drain water again and refill with cold fresh water. Let stand another 30 minutes.

Drain bowl and dry potato chips between two towels. Fry chips in deep fat until lightly browned. Drain on brown paper and sprinkle with salt. Saratoga chips!

NOTE: I used rendered beef tallow for the deep-fat frying. It took a lot of time, but the chips were excellent — a taste from way back in history. Have you ever eaten a real Saratoga chip?

CHAPTER 8

SOUP POOP

I am not calling soup a dirty name. *Poop*, a word that has been around for centuries, has many meanings. There's the raised stern deck of a ship, the poop deck; a foolish person, an old poop; the true facts of the case, the real poop. I'm using the word in the latter sense. I am giving you the facts about soup, accompanied by some of my experiences with soup and other things. Any other interpretation of the word is yours, and shame on you!

Soups have always been large in my life. As a baby I was fed on Cream of Wheat, which was darned near a soup the way Mother prepared it. Then I graduated to vegetable soup, which is what Mother called the soup in the pot that was always on the back of the stove. This was a sort of ongoing soup, as Mother would dip out of it for any meal and add to it any leftovers. Once a week

we emptied the pot, washed it, and started again.

I did as my father did in the early days. He'd go to the soup pot, dip out a cup of liquid and drink it, then add a cup of water to the pot. In effect I "had a V-8," hot, at an early age.

The dominant soup of my memory is clam chowder. There's no better way to feed a lot of people with a minimum of meat. The clams grew in our front yard, or what was our front yard when the tide went out. At low tide we needed only two buckets and a clam gun (special digging shovel) to dig up the makings of a big feed.

To the clams we added whatever else was available — bacon, potatoes, onions, canned milk. The water was free. Wood for the cooking fire, we cut on the mountain in our backyard. It was a happy place to live during those

Depression years. Few people were living in Alaska in those days, but the word spread and many discovered that Alaska was a land of opportunities.

The soups of this country tend to be full of meat and vegetables, one bowlful a meal in itself. That's no accident, as many people are fond of soup and all will eat it. During my traveling days I dipped a ladle into many a pot of soup, closely followed by a spoon in a bowl.

There are some notable exceptions. Once, in a camp of some Southeast Alaska Natives, I was offered my turn with the soup ladle. I approached the pot with skill and confidence. As I slid the pot cover to one side, I was nearly overcome by the delicious smell. Bouillabaisse, I guessed, but I found only salmon heads in the pot. As I eased the ladle into the liquid, the soup looked up at me with what was unmistakably an eye. Deftly I eased the eye to one side and dipped out a ladleful of liquid. I was about to empty the ladle into my bowl when the eye surfaced. What could I do? Well, I tipped the ladle and returned the eye to the pot with my spoon.

My host assured me that the eye was a delicacy to be cherished, and he carried it off, but the glint of fun in his eye made me doubt whether he was giving me the straight poop. The clear liquid of the soup was good enough to rate a second (eyeless) bowl.

And once in Ketchikan, also in Southeast Alaska, I was served a bowl of what looked like the cat's dinner — a bowl of hot milk with four dark objects floating in it. I commented jokingly about the absence of solid content and was abruptly informed that this was oyster stew, one of the world's great delicacies, rating just a hair under caviar. It was good, but how much better it would have been with more oysters and a few vegies!

Enough about seafood soups. I have found many real meat soups in my travels. The base was beef, moose, caribou, mountain sheep, or one of the staples such as hamburger, ham or bacon, or one of the meats I won't mention lest it upset you. The vegetable content was usually in direct relationship to how far it was to the nearest grocery store. The traditional soups might have been aimed at, and sometimes hit, but the originality demonstrated was admirable, especially in the far-out Bush locations.

If I seem to belabor the taste of mountain sheep, it does give soup a wonderful taste. I've experienced sheep stew, and sheep soup, which was different only in the size of the ingredients. Fantastic! I've always intended to try the recipe with mutton. Have a go at it if you dare.

Please don't get the idea that every soup I've dipped a ladle into was good soup. There are people out there who cannot create a good soup. My nose can usually detect a bad soup, and so I have escaped most of those. Connie kids me at times. "You may have missed a wonderful new taste treat out there." I always answer, "One has to leave something for future generations to discover."

Once, in a remote mining camp, I was waiting for a plane to come in and rescue me one more time. I was hungry enough to eat a bear — on the run if he refused to stand still for it. Four young men were working the claim, and they hadn't thought to hire or recruit someone who could cook, so they took turns. I was there on Ed's day. The odor of something in the cooking pot drew my nose and me to the cook tent. Ed informed me proudly that he was making porcupine soup, and he had caught the meat himself.

I eased over to the stove and lifted the cover from the pot. The steam whiffed out a smell that made my stomach cramp with anticipation. When the steam cleared I could see porcupine quills floating on the top of the liquid, and then a tiny, clawed foot broke the surface.

With consummate tact I asked Ed whether he had found it difficult to skin and clean the porcupine. He answered with a blank look. I smiled and started down the trail toward the airstrip. On the way I met the other three miners, hungry and headed for the cook tent. It seemed cruel to tell them what they would find, but I had no choice. It was

tell them now, or come back later to investigate a murder.

"I think he was pulling your leg, Trooper," Pete said with a grin. "Ed cooks up animals to feed his dog."

"Don't kill him," I said with a steely-eyed look. "I want the pleasure." I might have gone back, too, except that I saw the plane in its final approach.

Two days later I was back at the same mining camp. They hadn't killed Ed, but they sure had bent him some. We all went to town, and two of the four missed thirty days of the mining season. They ate better in jail.

I'm not discouraged by the poorer soup-making results I've encountered. If they have the attention span to boil water without burning it, ninety-five percent of all people can make a good soup. Throw a chicken into a pot of water for a start. Oops! Throw a defeathered, deheaded, declawed and deviscerated chicken into a pot of hot water. When the meat is falling off the bones you have the base for any one of a thousand delicious soups. Not only that, you have the best cure yet found for the common cold.

There are people who must go creative, and most of them do it with admirable results. There are those who can follow instructions faithfully, and it is for them that cookbooks are written. Be true to yourself, but don't reach for a can of soup! Please!

ALASKA'S PLENTY SOUP

The cooks in the nation's largest state are always looking for new ways to utilize the things it produces in abundance. Well, so far no one has come up with a recipe that includes North Slope oil, but I do think everything above ground has been at least considered. This recipe demonstrates utilization of our own ingredients, but with substitutes for elsewhere.

3 pounds spareribs of caribou,
    moose, pork, beef or
    whatever is available
1 1/2 pounds sauerkraut
    (canned if necessary)
3 cups chopped onions
3 tablespoons butter or
    margarine
3 tablespoons all-purpose flour
1 pound mushrooms or 2 4-ounce
    cans
1 bay leaf
1/2 teaspoon celery seed
1 teaspoon salt
pepper

In a large Dutch oven or covered soup pot, cover ribs with water and bring to a boil. Cover pot, reduce heat and simmer for 30 minutes. Add sauerkraut and simmer for 60 more minutes. When meat is tender remove the ribs and store them in the refrigerator. Return the pot to the heat and simmer until the liquid is reduced to about 4 cups.

In a frying pan over medium heat sauté onions in the butter until golden brown. Remove onions and set aside. Sprinkle flour into the butter, stir, and when flour is slightly browned add a cup of water, a bit at a time. Keep stirring. When mixture is smooth, add onions, mushrooms, bay leaf, celery seed and salt and pepper. Stir this mixture thoroughly into the stock and sauerkraut in the Dutch oven. Bring back to a boil, then reduce heat and simmer for another 60 minutes. Discard the bay leaf. Serves four.

Oh yes, the ribs. Try heating them the next day and painting them with Barbecue Sauce, on page 38.

Fantastic!

DILLINGHAM SPLIT PEA SOUP

Some years ago, in Dillingham on the west coast, I was served a different and interesting split pea soup. It had the distinct taste of dill. Where else but in Dillingham!

1 cup dry green split peas
1 cup peeled and finely diced
   carrots
1 cup finely chopped onions
2 quarts water
1 tablespoon soup base, ham
   flavor
1/2 teaspoon salt
1/4 teaspoon dried, minced
   garlic
1/2 teaspoon crushed dill weed
pepper

Bring water to a boil over medium heat, add all the other ingredients, stir well, cover and reduce heat. Simmer about 30 minutes, check and add more water if needed. Simmer 60 minutes, check again, add water if needed. Simmer another 60 minutes and you'll have a thick soup. Add pepper to taste. Serves four.

STEAMED EGG SOUP

This recipe creates something that acts more like custard than a soup. The note from the recipe's provider said the soup could be eaten as a meal starter or finisher. I found him right.

4 eggs
2 cups chicken stock (bouillon
   and water okay)
salt and white pepper
1 cup fresh shrimp, cut in pieces
   (or 1 6-ounce can tiny
   shrimp)
1 tablespoon minced green
   onions

In a heat-proof bowl that will fit into whatever steaming device you own, whip the eggs. Blend in chicken stock. Season with salt and pepper to taste. Add shrimp and onions and mix well.

Set bowl in the rack of your steamer over boiling water for 15 minutes. The custard-type contents should be just nicely set. Serve hot to two.

NOTE: I've substituted chicken pieces for the shrimp and found it excellent. Or you might try ham, fish or whatever you have available. Surprise someone.

KNIK BLACK BEAN SOUP

In my files are several recipes for cooking black beans, none of which I had tried. The reason was simple: no black beans. The other day I was wandering through the new health food section of a local supermarket. Behold, black beans. I scooped up a couple of pounds and ran home in the pickup truck to try cooking them. This was the first recipe I tried and there was no reason to go to another. It's great!

1 cup black beans
1 quart water
2 tablespoons ham soup base
    (or add a ham bone)
4 bay leaves
4 whole cloves
1/4 teaspoon celery seed
1 tablespoon vegetable oil
1 cup chopped onions
1 cup chopped celery, with
    leaves
2 garlic cloves, minced
1/4 teaspoon dry mustard
1 teaspoon medium chili powder
2 dashes hot sauce (Tabasco)
3 eggs, hard-cooked
1 cup cream, whipped

Soak beans overnight in water. Drain and put back 1 cup of the water. Add ham soup base or bone, bay leaves, cloves and celery seed. Cover and simmer at medium heat until beans are tender. Check occasionally and add small quantities of water if required. Check for doneness after 1 hour.

Add oil to a frying pan over medium heat and sauté onions, celery and garlic. Blend in mustard, chili powder and hot sauce. Add to cooked beans.

Put the bean soup through your blender, a bit at a time, until all has been puréed. If it doesn't appear thick enough add a tablespoon of butter blended with a tablespoon of flour and cook until it is thick.

Pour into bowls, scatter chopped hard-cooked eggs over the top of each bowl, top with a gob of whipped cream and serve. Serves four. It's a BINGO!

PORTUGUESE FISH SOUP

A visit to my brother brought me in contact with his next-door neighbors, a family of Portuguese heritage and proud of it. The soup I was served this day, and the recipe, stayed with me. The wife was puzzled that a man wanted a recipe, but willing to give it to me. Today I seldom cook beans without adding enough to save out two cupfuls. With those two cups I can make this soup the next day. Try it and you'll know why.

2 medium onions, chopped
1 garlic clove, minced
1 tablespoon vegetable oil
2 tablespoons all-purpose flour
6 cups hot water
1 cup chopped spinach, chard or
    whatever is in season
    (canned if necessary)
1 bay leaf
1 teaspoon paprika
1 dash hot sauce (Tabasco)
1/2 pound cubed cod (or any
    whitefish)
2 cups cooked white beans
salt and pepper

In a large pot over medium heat sauté onions and garlic in the oil. When onions are tender, sprinkle flour over them and stir until lightly browned.

Add water, spinach, bay leaf, paprika and Tabasco. Bring liquid to a boil, add fish, reduce heat and simmer for 8 minutes. Add beans and simmer 2 minutes until beans are hot. Remove bay leaf and season to taste with salt and pepper.

Serve hot to four hungry people.

MILDRED'S BAKED SOUP

Until the day Mildred slid a bowl of this soup in front of me, I had never even heard of baked soup. She grinned and said, "Top this, Mr. Cookbook Writer!" Being an expert in women, I kept my mouth shut and reached for a spoon. Yep! My intelligent handling of the situation earned you another recipe.

1/3 cup butter (margarine only if
    you have to)
1/2 cup sliced celery (1/4-inch
    slices)
1 cup chopped onions
2 teaspoons bacon, dry-fried and
    crumbled (or Bacon Bits)
1/3 cup all-purpose flour
1 teaspoon fresh or dried parsley
1 cup cooked and diced chicken
2 cups chicken stock (bouillon
    and water okay)
1 cup cream, whipped
grated Parmesan cheese
salt and pepper

In a large saucepan over medium heat melt butter and sauté celery and onions until tender. Add bacon and flour and stir until mixture is smooth. Add parsley.

Remove from heat and stir in the chicken and stock. When liquid is smooth return to heat and cook until soup comes to a boil.

Divide soup into 4 ovenproof bowls. Top with whipped cream. Sprinkle Parmesan cheese over whipped cream. Slide bowls, on a cookie tray, into the broiler, about 4 inches from the heat source. Watch carefully and the moment the cheese starts to melt remove from broiler and serve to four surprised people.

NOTE: Mildred never uses salt and pepper, but some people may prefer it. Season before the boiling stage. I've been known to add other leftover vegetables to this soup without doing any major damage to the taste.

ONION-LOVER'S SOUP

You haven't reached this stage in recipe-collecting without noticing I'm downright partial to onions. The moment this recipe fell out of an envelope I knew I was in heaven. The sender, too, had noted that I like onions and sent this to be my ultimate recipe. This person had all three of my books and had given many as gifts. With all that going for a recipe, of course I would try it.

4 tablespoons butter or
    margarine
2 cups chopped yellow onions
1 cup chopped red onions
1/2 cup chopped green onions
4 cups beef stock (bouillon and
    water okay)
1/2 teaspoon ground thyme
1 tablespoon dry crumbled
    parsley
salt and pepper
1 cup cream (evaporated milk
    okay)

Melt butter in a saucepan over medium heat. Add all the onions and sauté, stirring, until soft.

Add beef stock, thyme and parsley. Bring to a simmer and cook covered for 15 minutes. Salt and pepper to taste.

Strain resulting soup through a strainer, saving both solids and liquid. Put solids and 1 cup of liquid into the blender and purée. Pour purée back into remaining liquid.

Return to medium heat and slowly whisk cream into soup. When mixed, simmer for 5 minutes to blend the flavors.

Remove from heat and serve to four lucky onion-lovers.

NOTE: It's a BINGO all right, but my ultimate recipe is still out there someplace.

NONPOTATO CLAM CHOWDER

Make a clam chowder without potatoes, nonsense! Those little cubes of potatoes are what make it chowder. So this recipe was quickly relegated to my file thirteen. Then several hours later I found myself digging for it. The idea was interesting, even if ridiculous. Rose M., the sender, was a Nelson cookbook owner twice-over, thought they were wonderful, and was an onion-pusher. The recipe had a lot going for it right there. I'd try it.

2 10-ounce cans whole baby
    clams, with juice
2 cups chicken stock (bouillon
    and water okay)
1 cup chopped onions
3 garlic cloves, minced
2 tablespoons dried and
    crumbled parsley
1 cup dry vermouth
pepper, fresh, coarsely ground
    if possible
1/2 pound linguini

In a large saucepan combine clam juice, stock, onions and garlic. Cook at high heat for 5 minutes. Add parsley and vermouth and cool 5 minutes. Add pepper to taste and set aside, but keep warm.

In a second large pot bring water to a boil, add salt if you wish, and cook linguini as the package directs. When done, drain and add hot linguini to soup liquid.

Add clams to soup and heat just to eating temperature. Divide into 4 large soup bowls and serve to as many lucky people. The quickly emptied bowls will give you the vote of success or failure. I'll vote for the former.

CREAM OF CARROT SOUP

One spring day I moved something in the freezer and found more carrots than I knew we had. Carrot consumption would have to be increased. Carrot cake three times a week and carrots as a dinner vegetable twice a week wouldn't do it. Carrot soup? Craftily disguised? A recipe was born.

1 pound chopped carrots, fresh
    or surplus frozen
1 cup chopped onions
4 cups beef stock (beef bouillon
    and water okay)
1 teaspoon salt
1/4 teaspoon pepper
1 teaspoon sugar
1 4-ounce cube butter
1/2 cup flour
2 cups milk

In a large pan over medium heat combine carrots, onions, stock, salt, pepper and sugar. Bring to a boil, cover, reduce heat and simmer for 50 minutes.

In a saucepan melt butter and sprinkle in flour. Stir to a smooth paste and add milk gradually to create a white sauce. Extra milk can be used to reach the right consistency.

In your blender purée carrots and onions with their cooking liquid. Blend half the liquid at a time. Stir puréed carrot mixture into white sauce. Adjust seasoning if necessary and serve. Serves four to six.

ONE MORE BEET SOUP

In each of my cookbooks I have given my readers a beet soup, and this entry is to continue the tradition. It was one of the few recipes to come to me from a man. Women and couples send recipes often. It was simple, straightforward, and surprisingly good.

1 can sliced beets
1 13 1/2-ounce can beef stock
2 dill pickles, chopped
1 medium onion, chopped
3 tablespoons cider vinegar
black pepper, fresh, coarsely
*   ground*
1/3 cup sour cream

A blender is necessary to prepare this recipe. Put the undrained beets into the blender, followed by stock, pickles, onions and vinegar. Blend until contents are smooth. Add pepper and blend another few seconds.

Divide purée into 4 soup bowls and place in refrigerator to chill for an hour minimum. Remove and serve cold with a dollop of sour cream in each bowl. Serves four.

CHAPTER 9

PASTA NOW

When anyone gets me started talking about cooking, which isn't so easy as you may imagine, the subject of pasta is bound to come up. It is one of my favorite foods, as the variety and scope of the ingredients seem almost endless. People find material enough to write whole books about pasta, so I can certainly slip some new (for me) recipes into this book. Connie keeps saying I dream up a new pasta recipe every week. What she means is, I never make exactly the same dish twice. One forever seeks to make things better.

As far back as I can remember, I've seen cooks doing imaginative things with pasta. Few turn out to be masterpieces, but some of the failures are darned good. Any pasta covered with a reasonable sauce is good.

Out in Alaska's Bush country, where storage facilities in most households and camps are limited, pasta was what kept people fed. Well, there were beans, but we won't go into them here. Let the mercury drop to fifty below, or rise to a hundred above, pasta will survive. It's always ready to provide the filler that men require when they're doing hard outdoor work. Cook pasta, cover it with sauce, and men will eat it.

True, pasta can be overworked. The prime example of that, which I may have mentioned in previous books, is the one that sparked the revolt in a logging camp in the Southeast. There the excellent consommé royale had degenerated into an elbow-macaroni soup with little else in the water. The men ate it without complaint. Then came the day this soup was followed by macaroni salad plus macaroni and cheese.

As the salad was served the head logger rose. His name was Sven — a huge Scandinavian, six-foot-six and some 270 pounds. You could have heard an ax handle hit the floor when he stood up to speak. He announced that he was fed up with pasta, and he held a hand the size of a Ford wheel up to his eyebrow to show how fed up he considered himself to be.

The cook came out of the kitchen to see why it was suddenly so quiet in the mess hall. Sven pinned the cook to the wall with his eyes and spoke directly to him. "How much macaroni do you got in the kitchen?"

The cook glanced at the camp superintendent for support, but was left on his own. "About fifty pounds, I guess," he answered.

Sven smiled, or at least showed the cook his pearly white teeth, and said, "Cook, ven next you cook macaroni, cook it all, and make a good sauce, for you, my friend, are going to eat efry bite of macaroni that leafs your kitchen. Efry curly piece of it!"

Sven sat down and finished his macaroni salad. He was not one to waste food, even macaroni so long as it was cooked before he made his announcement.

I left the camp late the same evening and didn't get back for months. The pasta ban was still in effect and I heard some grumbling about the absence of consommé royale. Rice was the new standby, and everyone was waiting for Sven to deliver an edict against rice. He seemed to be enjoying it.

I asked some of the fellows how come the superintendent let Sven dictate to the company cook. The answer was simple. The super had talked to Sven, and got himself assigned to help eat the fifty pounds of macaroni if it showed up in the mess hall again. Dinner that night was hash.

I have another pasta dish that's fit for a king, or a couple of hungry hunters, but you won't find the recipe here. Feel free to try duplicating it if you must. It came about because, back in the early days, some of us toyed with the idea of "living off the country." That phrase was tossed around with great stupidity.

On this occasion three of us had been drifting down a river for three days, through a gameless waste. Not even a porcupine had shown its face. The grub box was down to a single can of peas and a pound of macaroni. Oh, yes, and a bit of salt, as the top of the shaker had come off and dumped the stuff into the grub box.

Evening came upon three hungry fellows. I can still remember the gnawing in my stomach, and the dread of crawling into my sleeping bag hungry. Then, out of the fading light, came a whistle. One of the guys yelled, "Duck!" and took off at a full run. A heavy rifle boomed nearby, and he yelled, "Got him!"

So that night we ate. Duck stew! A simple recipe: one duck, one pound of macaroni, one can of peas, a sweeping of salt and a lot of water. One of the most satisfying meals I can remember. I called it Consommé Duck Royale.

Before another night caught up with us we found civilization. Connie was sitting in the car beside a bridge over our river, with a basket of sandwiches and two thermoses of coffee. Now, there's a thinking wife. She had seen us "starve off the country" before.

During the years I was stationed in Juneau I had my cruiser rigged as a hand-troller, and I spent every possible summer day chasing the wily salmon. On one of those windy days when I should have stayed home, I found myself running into Hand Trollers' Cove seeking shelter. A larger ship lay at anchor there, and someone aboard held up a mug by the handle — an invitation to come aboard for a mugup. That's coffee and whatever. I went alongside and two fellows took my lines.

"Ed," the first one said as he offered me a hand to board. His partner extended his hand with "Pete." The preliminaries over, we ducked into the cabin out of the wind. The pot on the Shipmate stove was giving off a fantastic odor, and I hoped for an invitation to dinner. The cold and now soggy sandwiches aboard my *Connie II* had little appeal.

We talked fishing for a while. Ed and Pete were out after king crabs. Pete appeared to be the cook, and I watched hungrily as he lifted the cover of the pot, forked up a strand of linguini, and tested it between his teeth.

"Dinner," Pete said. "You'll stay?" I would!

Within a minute I was handed a plate heaping with pasta covered with a cream sauce. What a cream sauce! It was one-third king-crab chunks! More king crab than you'd ever see anywhere but aboard a boat with her hold full of them. It was fantastic. I had a second and wished I had room for a third.

That event ruined a theory I'd cherished for years — that crab fishermen do not eat crab aboard their ships. You know, I'd trade just about any of my cherished theories for another crab feed like that one.

Without a doubt the strangest use of pasta I've ever seen I also found in the Bush. I was armed with a bit of paper to serve on a man who lived in the Bush a hundred miles from Anchorage. He was thought to be in need of a psychiatric examination. He read the paper, snorted in disgust, and said, "Mugup? We'd better eat the apple pie before we go."

With the first bite I knew I'd found something unusual. The crust was made of elbow macaroni! It was good, and the filling was great. Between us we finished the pie in short order. I asked for the recipe and got only a grin. He was still grinning when I checked him into the hospital. If he was crazy, he was crazy like a fox.

GARLIC-LOVER'S SPAGHETTI

Not everyone loves garlic, although myth and modern scientific studies indicate that it's definitely a health food. I've never doubted that garlic helps to keep you healthy, but I have my own theory about why. If you smell of garlic, other people don't get close enough to you to transmit their germs and viruses to you. If you love garlic, but want to be close to your friends, male or female, I suggest you feed them garlic.

1 pound spaghetti
10 garlic cloves, peeled and finely
    minced
1 cup vegetable oil (preferably
    olive)
1/4 cup minced fresh parsley
1/2 teaspoon crumbled basil
1 dash cayenne
salt and pepper
1 cup grated Parmesan cheese

In a large cooking pot cook spaghetti as directed on the package. (Time varies with brand.)

In a frying pan over medium heat sauté garlic in oil until it just begins to change color. Add parsley, basil, cayenne and salt and pepper to taste. Blend well.

Drain cooked spaghetti and pour hot oil mixture over it. Toss until well-coated. Sprinkle with cheese and set more out for individual adding if desired.

Serves two to four.

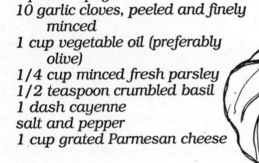

CANADIAN BACON AND PEA SPAGHETTI

This is one of the surprises a roadhouse on the Alcan Highway provided. I would not have ordered a pasta dish in a roadhouse or cafe, except I saw this delight served to another patron before I ordered. It was a fascinating array of colors. It was good, and here's my version of it. Just a tiny bit better.

1 4-ounce cube of butter
1 cup Canadian bacon strips
1 cup diced red pepper (canned if
    necessary)
1 package peas, fresh or thawed
    frozen
1/2 teaspoon salt
1/4 teaspoon black pepper
1 cup heavy cream (evaporated
    milk okay)
1 pound spaghetti or fettuccine
1 cup grated Parmesan cheese

In a frying pan over medium heat, melt butter and sauté bacon and peppers for 1 minute. Add peas and cook for about 2 minutes.

Salt and pepper mixture and add cream. Bring to a simmer and hold the temperature for 3 minutes while stirring. When the sauce thickens, set aside but keep warm.

Cook spaghetti as directed on the package, usually in a large pot of lightly salted boiling water for 8 to 12 minutes. Let the package set the time.

Drain cooked spaghetti and return to the pot. Pour in sauce and toss well to coat spaghetti strands. Sprinkle with cheese and toss again.

Serves four to six.

NOTE: Serving pasta on warmed plates is a nice touch. Substituting ham for Canadian bacon works well.

MARY ANN'S CHICKEN LINGUINI

Mary Ann is a lovely woman with only a few faults, one of which is she can't stand clams. There is something about the black tips of the necks which turns her off. I honor her right to dislike clams, but I pity her husband who loves Clam Linguini. He and I were down to Joe's place scarfing up clams when Mike said to me, "Give me a recipe for making this stuff, Gordy!"

"I can give you one for chicken linguini and you can substitute clams for chicken, okay? Mary Ann might even make it for you. You might like it!"

A month later Mike turned down my suggestion that we feed at Joe's place. "It's linguini night here. No! You are not invited. You devil, you knew your recipe was an aphrodisiac, didn't you?"

Now, when you've made a friend happy, you can't turn around and tell him it was all a mistake. So I chuckled in a manner most devilish and hung up.

1 pound chicken breast, boneless and skinless
1 egg, beaten
1 cup bread crumbs
1 teaspoon salt
1/2 teaspoon black pepper
1/2 cup vegetable oil
1 12-ounce package linguini
1 4-ounce cube butter or margarine
3 garlic cloves, minced
1 tablespoon lemon juice

It is advisable to prepare the chicken at least an hour before you assemble the dish. Cut chicken breasts into 1/2-inch strips. Dip pieces in beaten egg and roll them in a mixture of bread crumbs and salt and pepper. Lay the breaded pieces on a plate and refrigerate for an hour or more.

When it's time to cook, add oil to a frying pan over medium heat. Cook strips, half at a time. When pieces are golden brown, remove to a plate and keep warm. Discard oil and wipe out the frying pan.

Cook pasta as directed on the package.

Add all but 2 tablespoons of butter to frying pan and sauté garlic for 2 minutes. Add chicken pieces and toss to coat with garlic butter, but do not cook further. Remove to plate.

Drain pasta and add remaining butter to it. Toss to coat. Turn out onto a platter. Arrange chicken pieces around the platter. Add lemon juice to frying pan liquid and mix. Pour this sauce over pasta and serve.

Serves two to four. Recommend serving two only and live with the leftovers.

NUTS TO PASTA

An unusual recipe always attracts my attention. This one sure did, as I arrived at a friend's cabin after dinnertime and eighty miles from the nearest eating place. I went to my sleeping bag with a full stomach, thanks to this recipe. My host whipped it out in no time.

3/4 pound noodles (fettuccine suggested)
2 tablespoons butter
3 tablespoons crumbled dry basil (optional)
1/3 cup heavy cream (evaporated milk okay)
1/3 cup chopped nuts (pecans, walnuts, or other)
1/3 cup grated Parmesan cheese

Cook the noodles according to package directions, drain and save 1/2 cup of the cooking water. Pour it in the pan and add butter. Return noodles to cooking pan and toss to coat with butter.

Add basil, cream and nuts and toss again to blend. Turn out onto 2 or 4 individual serving plates. Divide the cheese among the portions. Serves two to four.

NELLIE'S
BREAKFAST
PASTA

Over the years I have often discussed the originality demonstrated by Alaska's roadhouse cooks in the early days. Usually working with limited supplies, they turned out good, wholesome, filling menus for traveling people. Connie and I sampled one like this on our honeymoon some forty years ago.

2 egg yolks
2 tablespoons honey
1 cup whole milk
3/4 teaspoon vanilla
1/2 cup salad macaroni, cooked
  by package instructions
cinnamon
1 11-ounce can mandarin orange
  slices

A double boiler is required to make this dish. To the top half add egg yolks and honey. Set over the bottom of the double boiler, filled with enough water to simmer over low heat.

In a second saucepan over medium heat, bring milk to just a scald. Add to honey-egg mixture and stir constantly until the custard thickens, about 15 minutes. Add vanilla and salad macaroni. Sprinkle with cinnamon.

Divide custard mixture between 2 serving bowls. Drain mandarin slices and top the custard. Serves two.

NOTE: From the time and energy needed to create this dish, you begin to realize what the early cooks went through to serve their customers.

RIO BRAVO MACARONI AND CHEESE

After casual comment to the effect that I had seen no evidence of the people below the border eating pasta, this recipe came in the mail. I still don't know its authenticity, but hey, it's good.

1 pound bulk pork sausage, hot
3 tablespoons butter or margarine
1 cup chopped onions
3 garlic cloves, peeled and minced
1/4 cup all-purpose flour
2 cups whole milk
3/4 teaspoon ground cumin
3/4 teaspoon salt
2 teaspoons crumbled oregano
2 tablespoons chili powder,
    medium
1 4-ounce can green chilies
1 4-ounce can olives, sliced
8 ounces elbow macaroni, cooked
    and drained
3 cups shredded Cheddar cheese

In a frying pan over medium heat cook sausage, crumbling it into small pieces as it browns. Remove and set aside on paper toweling to drain. Discard drippings left in the pan.

Put frying pan back over the heat. Add butter, onions and garlic and cook until onions are limp. Stir in flour and cook until the mixture is bubbly. Slowly add milk, stirring until it makes a smooth sauce and thickens. Remove from heat and add cumin, salt, oregano, chili powder, chilies and olives. Mix well and stir in drained pasta until well-coated with sauce.

Pour half the pasta and sauce into a greased baking pan, about 3-quart size. Add half the meat and half the cheese. Make a second layer of pasta, meat and cheese.

Bake in a preheated 400°F oven for 20 minutes or until the center of the dish is hot. Serve at once. Serves six.

VALDEZ ADVENTURE

The cook who first served me this dish didn't want to be remembered by some recipe called Spaghetti and Beans. So here you are, Gal. I hope you like the new name. Either way, it's good eating.

2 tablespoons vegetable oil (olive preferred)
1 cup chopped onions
1 cup ham cut in 1/4-inch cubes
3 garlic cloves, minced
1/4 teaspoon crumbled basil
1/2 teaspoon ground oregano
1 can Italian-style stewed tomatoes (liquid included)
1 quart chicken stock (bouillon and water okay)
1 15-ounce can kidney beans, drained
1/2 pound spaghetti, broken in thirds
salt and pepper
2 tablespoons chopped fresh parsley

In a large saucepan over medium heat combine oil, onions and ham. Sauté for 5 minutes and add garlic, basil and oregano. Cook another 2 minutes and add tomatoes and their liquid. Simmer another 4 minutes.

Add chicken stock and beans. Crush a few beans against the side of the pan to add body to liquid. Simmer for another 10 minutes.

Add 1/4 teaspoon salt and pasta to pot and simmer gently until pasta is cooked. Remove from heat and allow to sit covered, for 10 minutes.

Adjust salt and pepper to taste. Sprinkle with parsley just before serving. Serves four.

NOTE: This dish should always be a stew, so add water any time during the cooking if it begins to look too dry.

PASTA SHELLS
IN CREAM

I hate to shovel snow. I know, it's a terrible thing for an Alaskan of only 65 years to say. When I was 20, it wasn't so bad, but no longer. So you see, when I went to the cupboard with my mouth set for spaghetti and found we were out of it, I was most unhappy. I was left with two choices: shovel the car out of the snow and go to the store, or cook a pound of pasta shells for dinner. The shells won hands down. All was not lost, as I came out of it with a new recipe for you.

1 16-ounce package medium pasta
    shells
1 garlic clove, peeled and minced
1 4-ounce cube butter or margarine
1 package broccoli spears, cooked
    and cut into 1/2-inch pieces
1 cup heavy cream (or evaporated
    milk)
1/2 pound ham, cooked and
    slivered (or meat available)
2 eggs, hard-cooked and coarsely
    chopped (boiled, or fried and
    cut into chunks)
1 cup grated Parmesan cheese
    (maybe Cheddar?)

Cook pasta as directed on the package.

In a frying pan over medium heat sauté garlic in butter for 1 minute. Add broccoli and stir in cream. Add ham and egg chunks. Cook for 3 minutes. Mix in cheese and stir until it's melted.

Drain pasta shells and add them to sauce. Turn out into a serving dish. Serves four to six.

SWISS SAUSAGE AND PASTA

This recipe has a history — from some unknown German woman living in Pennsylvania, to my great-grandmother, to a grandmother, to a mother, to a son — me! I'm sure each individual made some changes in the recipe. It may be as full of holes as the Swiss cheese included in the present-day version. One thing is for sure, it survived in good shape and fills stomachs as well as it did in the early 1800s. A girl from Ireland met a girl from Germany and became friends as well as mothers of a growing nation.

*3/4 pound Polish or garlic
    sausage, very thinly sliced
4 tablespoons butter or margarine
2 cups chopped onions
3 tablespoons all-purpose flour
2 cups whole milk
4 teaspoons German or Dijon
    mustard
1/2 teaspoon caraway seeds
    (optional)
3/4 teaspoon salt
1/4 teaspoon black pepper
1/2 pound elbow macaroni
3 cups shredded Swiss cheese*

Brown sausage slices in 1 tablespoon of butter, in a large frying pan over medium heat. Lift and set aside.

Add remaining butter and onions to the pan. Cook until onions are limp. Stir in flour and cook until bubbly. Keep stirring and add milk slowly to create a smooth sauce, about 3 minutes. Remove from heat and stir in mustard, caraway seeds, salt and pepper.

In a large saucepan, cook pasta according to package instructions. When cooked, drain and add to sauce. Stir well.

In a shallow baking pan, about 3-quart size, spoon in a layer of sauce and pasta. Add a layer of sausage slices and a layer of cheese, using about half of each. Add another layer with cheese at the top.

Bake uncovered in a 400°F oven for 20 minutes. The center of the dish must be hot. Remove from oven and serve at once. Serves four to six.

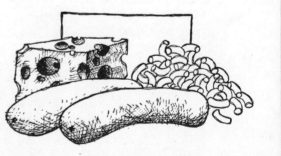

CHAPTER 10

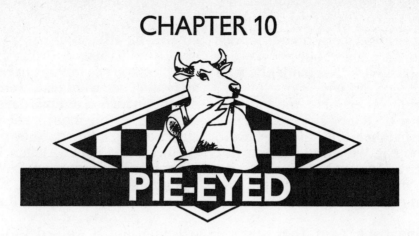

PIE-EYED

Way back in my youth, *pie-eyed* meant drunk. That made about as much sense to me as the alternative, *drunk as a skunk.* My older brother explained that an intoxicated person sometimes has trouble getting his eyes to track together, so each looks in a different direction. He could never explain the "skunk" reference to me, yet I pretended to understand.

To me a pie-eyed person should be one who's watching pies cooling on a windowsill. For housewives of older times, that was the place to cool pies. I learned from experience that going beyond the watching stage could be hazardous to your health. Temptation and maybe a dare made a criminal out of me. I and my buddy could eat a pie, scatter a few chunks and the pan under the window, and let the neighbor's dog take the blame.

My mother caught us with pie on our faces. My buddy, fair-weather friend that he was, took off on a dead run. He had somewhere to go. I didn't. My trial was speedy. Mother was the prosecutor and Dad, who would have shared in the pie, was the judge. Neither was amused, and I had difficulty sitting down for a while as a consequence.

My fair-weather friend didn't get out of it scot-free. After our brief discussion and fight when we met again, he was pie-eyed — one eye black and swollen and the other avoided looking at me for a week. Then we made up and were buddies again.

When I watched pies during their construction period, it was Mother who was pie-eyed. She never looked at a recipe, she just looked at the ingredients. Every pie she made was from scratch, as they call it now. Her apple pies bordered on divine, but she was more famous for her custard pie. I've often wondered whether it was the boat eggs that made them so good. Boat eggs did have more flavor.

When whipped cream came into our lives, Mother tried it on her custard pie. We convinced her that the pies were better without it. We did allow her to put whipped cream on pumpkin pies.

Now I'm hungry again! Just thinking of pies can do it.

Thinking back over the years, I believe the strangest pie I was ever offered was in a mining camp. Six men and a cook were working a claim, moving as much sand, gravel and (they hoped) gold through the sluice boxes as possible. Only during four months of the year could they work the ground; it was frozen the rest of the time. They were working fourteen-hour days.

One of the miners had been involved in a disturbance in a bar in Anchorage, and I had to interview him. My friendly Bush pilot dropped me on the gravel-bar landing strip, promised to return, and disappeared in the sky. We were having about twenty hours of daylight and four of dim light, so his return could be hours away.

The cook tent was on a gravel bar beside a rushing stream. I walked over, was offered a mugup at once, talked to the cook for a while, then wandered up to the work area. My actual work in the camp took all of thirty minutes.

Back at the cook tent, I watched the cook build what he called mincemeat pies. The main ingredient appeared to be meat, cooked and diced

small. The other ten percent was diced apples and raisins. Either he deliberately hid the seasonings or he was fast, as I didn't see what else went into the filling. He turned out two deep-dish pies designed to be main-meal dishes or sliced cold for lunch. They were out of the oven and cooling when I heard an aircraft engine overhead. Darn! I wasn't going to get a sample!

I was wrong. The cook cut a generous slice of pie and wrapped it in paper toweling, and I walked to the airstrip juggling the hot pie. The pilot took one look at what I had in my hands and said, "Damn! If I had known it was pie day over there, I'd have had a sudden attack of engine trouble. Good, isn't it!"

It was difficult to answer with my mouth full, so I nodded. I thought of suggesting he could still develop engine trouble, but I had duty elsewhere and duty won. I've tried several times to recreate "Leftover Pie," but never with that camp cook's success.

It's time to tell you about Mary Ann, who shall go without a last name to protect the guilty. Something about her attracted me at once. Maybe I was tasting love for the first time. It was bitter. She always had a few boys hanging around her, and all I got were a few wonderful dances with her. She floated like a feather in your arms. Graduation from high school separated us, and then the U.S. Army dominated three years of my life. Back in Anchorage as a civilian, I discovered that Mary Ann didn't live there anymore.

Ten years passed before I ran into her again, behind the counter in the small post office of another town. I spoke my name and she looked up with a start. "You were in my graduating class in high school! I'm Mary Ann."

Frankly, I never would have known. This Mary Ann was no longer light as a feather. I almost said so, but I bit my tongue and asked her out to lunch. We had apple pie in a cafe close by, and talked about school days. As she toyed with her pie she said, "I baked several of these, back then, hoping you would ask me to go out. You never did! You brought other girls and broke my heart."

"You always had a date."

"Only because you never asked me."

"Only because I assumed you were already spoken for away ahead."

"Silly kids, yes?"

"You were the prettiest girl in the class."

"No longer. I heard you're married and have a raft of kids. Who was she?"

"She was an eighth-grader when we graduated. We have several kids. You?"

"Married twice and divorced twice. Good men are hard to find."

"So are good women, Mary Ann."

"And you found one, right?"

"Yes, I was one of the lucky guys!"

I have never run into Mary Ann again in all my wandering about the state. I wasn't looking for her, either. My wife, Connie, makes excellent banana cream pies. I have three daughters who all make good pie crust and pies as well, and three sons who can eat pies right along with their father. It all works out for the best.

UNLIMITED PIE CRUST #1, #2 & #3

Over the years, I have known many people who absolutely could not make a decent pie crust. For them, the modern pie-crust mixes and even refrigerated pie crusts in a package are a lifesaver.

Not wanting to leave you at the mercy of modern technology and unable to fend for yourself in the battle for successful pastry, we offer you three recipes. Use freely with the recipes for fillings to follow.

Crust #1 (Basic)

4 tablespoons butter (preferably unsalted)
1 1/2 tablespoons solid shortening
1 cup flour
1/4 teaspoon salt
3 tablespoons ice-cold water

To begin, you must have butter and shortening well-chilled. Cut it up into 1/2-inch pieces.

Combine flour and salt in a large bowl. Cut in the chilled shortening and butter with a pastry blender, two forks or your own two hands. Work only until the mixture appears as a coarse meal.

Slowly add ice water until the dough forms into a ball. It might require only two tablespoons of water. If so, stop adding extra water right then. Wrap ball of dough in plastic wrap and refrigerate for 30 minutes.

On a lightly floured board, roll dough until it is 1/8-inch thick. Fold in half and transfer to a pie pan. Mold to the pan and trim the edges. Refrigerate still another 30 minutes.

To bake, press foil over the crust and fill evenly with pastry weights or dried beans. Bake in preheated 400°F oven for 15 minutes. The crust edges should just be turning brown. Take from oven and remove foil and weights. Poke several holes through the bottom of the crust and return to the oven for 10 to 15 minutes. It should be golden brown.

This is the crust to use for a pie that does not require further cooking, just fill and serve. It can also be used for pies requiring a limited time in the oven. It's for a one-crust-only pie.

Crust #2 (Cream, Custard or Quiche)

The basic directions are the same as for #1. Only the amounts of the ingredients are changed.

1 4-ounce cube butter
2 tablespoons solid shortening
1 1/4 cups all-purpose flour
1/4 teaspoon salt
5 tablespoons ice-cold water
    (again, use only as much as
    needed)

Crust #3 (Dessert pies)

The basic directions are much the same as for the other two. Mix sugar with flour and salt before adding shortening.

6 tablespoons butter
2 teaspoons white sugar
1 cup all-purpose flour
1/4 teaspoon salt
1 egg yolk
water (only if needed)

The egg yolk should be all the liquid needed to make the dough, but use water sparingly if necessary.

NELSON RHUBARB CUSTARD PIE

The northwest corner of my garden furnished the rhubarb for this pie. It grows huge and tall in the long summer days in Alaska. We've had so much I've even tried making wine out of it. It makes better pies! This is my mother's favorite recipe, the one I loved so as a kid. And still do! Lucky me!

3/4 cup honey
4 cups rhubarb, diced into
    1/2-inch chunks
3 eggs
2 pie crust #3 (bottom and top)
1/8 teaspoon ground nutmeg

Combine honey and rhubarb in a bowl and stir to coat every piece with honey. Set aside for an hour.

In a bowl, beat eggs and pour into rhubarb bowl. Mix well and pour into the bottom pie shell. Sprinkle with nutmeg. Add top crust and seal edges by fluting them. Cut several slashes for steam to escape.

Bake in a preheated 400°F oven for 10 minutes. Reduce the heat to 350°F and bake another 45 minutes.

Remove and let cool. Serve to four to six people.

NON-AIRPORT STRAWBERRY PIE

In the City of Anchorage, near the airport known as Merrill Field, there is a cafe. Way back in the 1950s, when I was learning to fly, this was where we went to renew our nerves and determination. I remember walking back there from my first aircraft crash. I sat at the counter and had coffee and strawberry pie. The pie was as near heaven as I had wanted to get so soon after looking death in the face.

In those days they cut a quarter of a pie as a serving. The other day I stopped in for the memories and was served an eighth of a pie at six times the price. Memories are so expensive these days! It sent me searching for a good strawberry pie recipe. How about this one?

2 pints fresh strawberries, hulled
*   and cleaned*
1 cup water
2/3 cup white sugar
1/4 cup cornstarch
food coloring
1 baked 10-inch pie crust #1
whipped cream

Separate one cup of strawberries, the small and imperfect ones. Crush these and add a cup of water. Simmer in a pan over medium heat for 2 minutes. Pour into sieve and allow all the juice to drain. Discard pulp.

Combine strawberry juice, sugar and cornstarch in a pan over medium heat. Bring to a boil and cook until liquid thickens. Add food coloring to the degree of red desired. Let mixture cool.

Slice remainder of strawberries. Place a layer in bottom of pie shell. Add half the sauce over this layer. Add remainder of strawberries and then remainder of sauce. Slide pie into the refrigerator to chill.

An hour or so later, remove, slice into quarters and serve to four people. Or two people twice, or one person four times. With lots of whipped cream.

LA TOUCHE
FRYING PAN PIE

One summer day in 1934, I was aboard the cannery tender *Pioneer*, out of Cordova. We ran in and hid from a storm near La Touche, a ghost town from an old mining operation. While several of us went ashore and explored the town, the cook stayed aboard and whipped up something different for dessert at evening chow. This is what he created:

3 tablespoons butter
1/4 cup water
1 1/2 cups white sugar
6 fresh apples, any kind, cored
*   and peeled*
1/2 teaspoon ground cinnamon
1 pie crust #3

You will need a 10-inch cast-iron frying pan or one of the new ovenproof glass ones. Over medium heat, combine butter, water and sugar. Cook until sugar is dissolved and the liquid is bubbling.

Slice apples in half and add halves to bubbling liquid. Turn often until apples are translucent and syrup is thick. Remove apples, turn them cut-side down, and sprinkle with cinnamon. Set aside to cool for an hour.

Roll out crust into a circle slightly larger than the frying pan. Transfer to pan and tuck down inside edges of the pan. Cut several vents in crust.

Bake in preheated 425°F oven for 20 to 25 minutes until the crust is golden brown. Remove from oven, cool and loosen crust from pan. Invert onto a serving plate. Cut into quarters and serve to four.

ALASKAN CHESS PIE

My recipe files are full of recipes for chess pie, and none have really appealed to me. Some even go back to the "half egg shell for tablespoon" time in cooking history. Then one day the airlines started flying direct to Hawaii, our sister state. This brought us macadamia nuts, and a new ingredient for chess pie. I gave it a try.

1 pie crust (your recipe or one of mine)
1 1/2 cups white sugar
2 tablespoons all-purpose flour
1 1/2 teaspoons grated lemon peel
5 eggs
1/4 teaspoon lemon juice
1 1/2 teaspoons vanilla
1/3 cup melted butter
3/4 cup chopped macadamia nuts (or your choice)
1/2 pint whipping cream

Start by rolling out a pie crust to fit a 9-inch pie pan. Make it large enough to turn under and crimp the edges. Chill crust while mixing filling. Preheat oven to 325°F.

In a large bowl, or your mixer bowl, combine sugar, flour and lemon peel. Beat into this mixture the eggs, one at a time. Add lemon juice and vanilla and continue mixing. Add melted butter slowly while mixing.

Pour mixture into pie shell and slide into the oven for about 30 minutes. Remove, sprinkle half the nuts into the filling, add a tablespoonful of nuts to the top and return to the oven for another 30 minutes. The filling should be firm and the top layer of nuts golden color.

Cool on a rack. When pie is cool, whip cream and spread on top, sprinkle the few remaining nuts on whipped cream and serve. Serves four to six.

NOTE: You are sure to have requests for seconds. Better make two pies right from the start.

BUSH COUNTRY COCONUT PIE

Many of the villages and out-lying areas get their groceries just once a year, with only a few emergency and fresh foods flown in at other times. When people out there suddenly develop a "Want!," they have to use their imagina-tions. I'm sure this recipe could have come from such conditions. It's either this or a snowbound cook in some other state. Several of them outdo us in snowfall and miserable weather.

Most of these ingredients are canned, powdered or dried in some way to give them a longer shelf life. Feel free to substitute better items if available.

3 eggs
2/3 cup white sugar
1 cup packed brown sugar
2/3 cup rolled oats, quick or
    other
2/3 cup shredded coconut
1/3 cup milk, or powdered mixed
    with water
1 teaspoon vanilla
1 tablespoon butter or margarine,
    melted
1 pie crust #1

In a large bowl beat eggs. Stir in sugars, oats, coconut, milk and vanilla. Add melted butter. Pour into pie crust.

Bake in a preheated 350°F oven for 30 minutes. Cool and serve to four to six.

NOTE: It's even better with whipped cream. You might try chilling and whipping a can of evaporated milk, just to see how they do it in the Bush.

CHOCOLATE CHIP AND APPLE PIE

This is one of those recipes that develop out of a lucky accident. I was about to build a Fudge-Apple pie but discovered I was out of baking chocolate. The Matanuska wind was whistling by at seventy knots and the road was drifting shut. I wasn't even tempted to go to the store. I rummaged around and found my supply of chocolate chips. We were in business.

2 cups cored, peeled and sliced
    apples
1 pie crust, #2
1/3 cup semisweet chocolate
    chips
2 eggs, separated
1 4-ounce cube butter, room
    temperature
2 teaspoons vanilla
1/3 cup all-purpose flour
1/2 cup white sugar
1/2 cup brown sugar

Spread apples evenly in pie crust. Sprinkle chocolate chips over apples. Set aside.

In a mixer bowl, combine egg yolks, butter, vanilla, flour and sugars. In a smaller bowl, beat egg whites until stiff peaks form. Fold egg whites into the other mixture. Spoon batter evenly over fruit. Smooth the top gently.

Bake in a preheated 375°F oven for 35 to 40 minutes. Test with a toothpick to see whether apple slices are done. It should come back clean.

Serve either warm or cold. I prefer warm with ice cream. Serves up to six, but four is best.

CHAPTER 11

WED AND BREAD

During the years between graduation from high school and getting married, I cooked little and baked even less. Instead I spent the years chasing women and serving in the United States Army. Any veteran of World War II in Alaska will tell you the former preoccupation was impossible during this period of time. A zillion soldiers and so few women.

For a brief time after December 1941, I was living with my folks in Kodiak. It was a town where the U.S. Navy had entered into the competition for available women. I'm afraid I was not used to such fierce competition and I had few dates during this period. So it was back to Anchorage and my pre-war stomping grounds. It was during the few short months when the Army had descended upon Anchorage. Never let it be said the Army took a back seat in the pursuit of

happiness. It is possible my being a hometown man was an advantage for a short time.

Suddenly it became evident that many nervous parents were sending their daughters to the Lower Forty-Eight in numbers high enough to ruin the hunting. Some were nervous about the war and the Japanese, but at least an equal number were worried about U.S. soldiers. By this time I was one of the latter group.

My future wife was a member of the shipped-out group, although I didn't know her then. What graduating senior pays any attention to a girl in the eighth-grade band? Her mother stayed to face the enemy, but Connie was shipped out.

My mind was preoccupied for some six weeks with the tired-out soldiers of the 4th Infantry basic training unit at Fort Richardson. I was one of those fellows with the close-cropped hair and two left feet.

Through hard work, determination and some degree of luck, I was finally assigned to a detachment on Fort Richardson. I was officially overseas, being across Ship Creek from the city of Anchorage, three miles from home. The spelling of the creek's name is correct, and I had a paddle.

It wasn't long after arriving in my detachment that I discovered the Class A pass. It allowed me to continue my search for girls. By now I had experienced the military vocabulary changes and learned a lot of new words. I thought of girls as women. I went to town the first time on my Class A pass with only one worry. Would I slip and let some more of my newfound vocabulary spill forth from my formerly careful mouth on my first date with a nice girl? No! Woman!

Things didn't go too well in the chase scene, although I managed a couple of dates during the next six months. Two weeks before Christmas in 1944, I committed the sin of all sins. I lost my Class A pass. I reported the loss faithfully to my first sergeant.

It was the day I discovered why our big, husky, hard-running commanding officer wasn't leading a company in Europe. I stood in front of his desk and heard him rule, "Soldier, you will not be issued a new Class A pass until such time as you find your old one!"

The fact that if I found my old one I wouldn't need a new pass didn't seem to make a connection in his mind. Not to mention that if I lost my pass in Anchorage and I was at Fort Richardson unable to go to the city, my chances of finding the old pass were nil. I never did under-stand how he made captain. I knew why he was in Siberia — excuse me, Alaska.

So, three miles from home, I joined the group of other soldiers who couldn't go home for Christmas. I helped cuss the commanding officer. Quietly, in the barracks where he couldn't hear. On Christmas Eve the others were encouraging me to go home on the "Burma Trail," the way to town where no passes were needed. I was tempted and who can say what might have happened after lights out. Yet something held me back.

I was deeply involved in a poker game at 2330 on Christmas Eve when the squawk box said, "Sergeant Nelson, report to the orderly room." I folded my pair of deuces I had planned to make a killing with and walked sedately to the orderly room. There was no use running; I wasn't going any place. I did put my tie back on as I walked.

I found the captain alone in his office, so I went in and tossed him a highball salute. He gave me back one of his infantry best, and shoved a Class A pass across the table to me. "Merry Christmas!" he said and smiled, slightly.

I said "Thanks!," tossed him another highball and took off for the barracks on a dead run. It would be a tight squeeze to catch the midnight bus. As I changed into my best uniform, I told the guys what happened.

Most of them thought the captain had the Christmas spirit for sure. One old staff sergeant, our platoon leader, had an interesting comment, "Yeah! But if Nelson had gone the Burma Trail, and not been here, he would have loosed the dogs and they would have had a nice hunt. He thinks you are fair game for anything, being a local resident."

The captain had waited awfully late before calling for me. I guess there are often two sides to any situation, but all I cared about was that I was headed for town. Even without a date, it was great to be free for a while.

Then came the night I went to a dance at the Gay Club. Whoa! Don't get ahead of me! At that time the word meant happy, excited. Well, it does startle people to mention, now, how I met my wife at the Gay Club. Yet that is what happened. This cute little blonde bombshell had everyone lining up to dance with her. The best I could do was find out her name was Connie.

She was back from visiting relatives in Oregon. She was enjoying herself and she couldn't see me for the similarity of my uniform to thirty others at the dance.

Yet that same night I discovered another girl. She was a husky Scandinavian girl who loved to dance the schottische and polka in the mode I grew up with. The one that uses up a lot of floor space. We went flying around the hall with great abandon.

We may have knocked her down or something, but we caught Connie's attention with our gyrations. She loved to dance like that, too. Through the next few weeks we found ourselves in the same clique of dancers. We often danced the slower and more sedate dances together. I'm of course referring to jitterbugging, Swedish waltzes and such. She was fun to dance with.

One night my usually vigorous dancing partner was at home with a cold. I was about to sit out a schottische when suddenly Connie was standing in front of me. We flashed onto the floor with the usual abandon of the dance. This gal was fantastic. I began to think she was fantastic off the floor as well. I was falling in love.

I walked her home one evening after a dance and asked her to marry me. Much to my surprise, she said "Yes!" It was her mother who said "No!" Connie was seventeen and her mother said no marriage until she was eighteen. I think her mother hoped we would both change our minds. See, Helen, it's lasted forty-one years, this love and marriage.

Connie has always said I looked scared waiting at the altar for her, so she winked at me. It made me grin and everyone commented on how my face lit up when I saw Connie. My heart did flip as I saw her, but I had tight control on my emotions right up until the wink. I've always been glad she did it.

Suddenly we were a couple living in a garage with a double bed and everything. A month later we moved into a brand-new rented home. It had a stove with an oven and we were back cooking and baking.

A year later we had the first section of our own home built and were moving into it. We also had a pretty little girl named Lauralee, and suspected another was on the way. Anyone mentioning a "bun in the oven" then would have been picking up his scattered teeth, but now I've mellowed.

In fact, at the drop of a hat I'll pop a batch of buns into the oven, set out the butter, and start slicing the onions. I've always been a bread lover. No! Don't say it!

NO-BOX
SUNDAY
HOT BREAD

STOP! Do not reach for the packaged, one-batch, hot bread mix. Yes, I know, it's quick and easy, but do you know what is in that package? I don't either, but I know what goes into this recipe. It's been around for a hundred years or so, so it can't be too bad, either to make or to eat.

3/4 cup white sugar
2 tablespoons butter or
      margarine
1 egg
1 cup milk
1 teaspoon lemon extract
1 1/2 cups all-purpose flour
3 teaspoons baking powder
1 pinch salt
cinnamon and sugar

In a large bowl cream sugar and butter together. Beat egg into milk and add to butter and sugar mixture. Add lemon extract, flour and baking powder. Oh yes, a pinch of salt as well. Mix well.

Pour mixture into a lightly greased 10-by-13-inch flat baking pan. Sprinkle the top with cinnamon and sugar.

Bake in a preheated 375°F oven for 25 to 30 minutes. Remove from pan and cut into pieces. Serve hot with lots of butter. Maybe a touch of strawberry jam.

NOTE: Try it for a Sunday morning breakfast. I doubt if you will have any leftovers.

CONNIE'S PUMPKIN BREAD

This is a recipe my wife discovered during the Christmas baking season of 1982. She sampled a friend's bread and used the Nelson technique to pull the recipe from a reluctant cook involved. I congratulate her on her effort. (She loves these little notes when she's proofreading my writing.)

2/3 cup solid shortening
2 2/3 cups sugar
4 eggs
1 16-ounce can pumpkin
2/3 cup water
2 teaspoons baking soda
1/2 teaspoon baking powder
1 1/2 teaspoons salt
3 1/3 cups all-purpose flour
1 1/8 teaspoons ground
    cinnamon
1 1/8 teaspoons ground cloves
2/3 cup raisins
2/3 cup chopped nuts, your
    choice

In a large mixing bowl combine shortening and sugar. Add eggs, pumpkin and water and mix well. Blend in baking soda, baking powder, salt and flour. Add cinnamon, cloves, raisins and nuts. Mix well.

Grease the inside bottoms of 3 loaf pans (4 1/4 by 8 1/2-inch size, 2 1/2-inches deep). Pour dough evenly among the 3 pans.

Bake in a preheated 350°F oven for about 60 minutes. Check with a toothpick. Out clean is done. If necessary, add 15 minutes to baking time.

Remove from oven and cool slightly. Run a knife around edges and remove loaves for further cooling. They should be about room temperature before slicing. Otherwise, they will crumble.

Serve as dessert, snack or whatever.

McDUFF'S FLOT BROD (Flat bread)

The McDuff who baked this bread is no longer with us. For years he lived alone on one of the tributaries of the Susitna River, a bit west of my place. He claimed he didn't like people, but what he really meant was he didn't like crowds of people. I always found him hospitable and ready for a visit when I dropped in at his place. Yet I was the Trooper covering his area. I always got a mugup of coffee or tea and something he had baked. He'd set a brown paper bag of flot brod on the table and say, "Help yourself." Then he'd shove a jar of strawberry jam or sometimes peanut butter my way. Here's what he made for himself and an occasional guest:

2 1/2 cups all-purpose flour
1/2 cup whole wheat flour
1/2 teaspoon salt
*1/4 cup shortening (McDuff
  favored bear fat)*
1/4 cup butter or margarine
1 1/4 cups hot water
2/3 cup cornmeal
1/3 cup all-purpose flour

In a large bowl combine 2 1/2 cups all-purpose flour with whole wheat flour. Add salt and cut in shortening and butter. Mix to a coarse meal consistency. Add hot water and stir with a spoon until well-mixed. Cover bowl tightly and cool overnight. McDuff would set his outside in a bear-proof box he had built. A refrigerator will do.

Next day take off the cover. Combine cornmeal and 1/3 cup flour and sprinkle on a mixing board. Pinch off egg-size pieces of chilled dough and pat on each side in cornmeal mixture. Roll pieces out as thin as possible, pressing the meal into dough. Set aside while you create more strips from the rest of the dough.

Place your ungreased frying pan on the stove and get it very hot. Cook the pieces, a few at a time, 2 minutes to each side. The dough will dry and bubbles will appear on either side. Remove to a rack and cool while you finish the other pieces.

When your rack is full, slide it into preheated 350°F oven for about 4 minutes. The bread will turn nicely brown and crisp. Serve it hot with butter and other things. Keep it in a paper sack and it will be good a week later as well. Makes about 20 flot brod.

MR. SMITH'S BREAD

I got this recipe from a friend, Mr. Smith. I call it "monkey bread" because while I was making it, I was watching a program on television about an unusually intelligent simian and his adventures in Washington, D.C. The act should not be construed as a political comment. Unless you absolutely have to.

1 1/4 cups milk, room
    temperature
3 tablespoons white sugar
1 teaspoon salt
1 package dry yeast
2 eggs
3 1/2 cups all-purpose flour
6 ounces butter or margarine,
    room temperature
8 ounces butter or margarine,
    melted

In a large bowl combine 1 cup of milk, sugar, salt and yeast. Add eggs and beat. Add remaining milk and flour and mix thoroughly. Cut in room-temperature butter and blend into dough. Turn out onto a floured board and knead until smooth. Cover with damp cloth and let rise until double in size. Knead again and let rise for 40 minutes.

Roll dough into a long log or roll. Cut into 28 pieces of equal size.

Butter and flour 2 9-inch tube pans. Roll each piece of dough into a ball and then roll it in the melted butter. Place 14 balls in each pan, 7 in the bottom layer and 7 in the top layer. Set both pans in a warm place to rise again.

When the pans are nicely filled and heaped above, brush the top layer with butter again. Slide into a preheated 375°F oven. Bake for 15 minutes, until the top is nicely browned.

Remove from oven, slip bread from pans, let cool for 10 minutes and serve. Serves many hungry people, with usually a few leftovers.

NOTE: As our family shrank I reduced the recipe in half. Still, the bread disappeared rapidly. People can smell it for blocks. Far distant neighbors may come over to get acquainted. Mugup time!

TONI'S GRAHAM BREAD

Toni was my mother's nickname and is now my middle daughter's real name. She was born on my folks' anniversary. As long as Mother lived, she whipped out a few loaves of graham bread each week. I've long suspected it was the binder that kept my parents together for a lifetime. Try this one!

2 3/4 cups warm water
1/4 cup shortening
1/3 cup molasses (or honey)
1 1/2 teaspoons salt
1 package dry yeast
3 cups white flour
3 cups graham flour

In a large bowl combine warm water, shortening, molasses and salt. Cool to lukewarm and dip out a 1/4 cup of liquid. Add yeast to this cup and let stand for 5 minutes.

Pour yeast liquid into a large bowl. Add 3 cups of white flour and 2 1/2 cups of graham flour to the bowl. Mix flour mixture into bowl of molasses liquid. Now add remaining 1/2 cup of graham flour and mix again. Cover and set in a warm place to rise.

When doubled in bulk, punch down again and divide the dough evenly into 2 well-greased bread pans. (Or do as Mother often did, shape the 2 sections of dough into 2 round free-standing loaves on a cookie sheet.)

Bake in a preheated 375°F oven for 45 minutes. Use the thump test for doneness. Cool on wire racks.

Eat one loaf warm with butter and thinly sliced onions. Save the other loaf for later.

MOTHER NELSON POPOVERS

My mother used to make something she called popovers. She learned the recipe as a girl and I guess she never jotted it down, as I couldn't find it. Over my years of cookbook writing, a half-dozen popover recipes have come from you out there. This is what I've gleaned from all of them. These taste like Mother's.

1 cup all-purpose flour
1/4 teaspoon salt
1 tablespoon melted butter or
*   margarine*
1 cup milk, room temperature
2 eggs
vegetable oil

Start by preheating the oven to 450°F. Then slip in well-oiled popover or muffin pans. Heat them for 5 minutes while you mix the batter.

In a bowl sift flour and salt together. In another bowl combine butter and milk. Pour mixture into flour bowl while stirring. Beat eggs in a third bowl and add to mixture.

Pour the batter into hot popover pans, each cup about 2/3 full. Dust lightly with flour and slide into hot oven. Bake 15 minutes at 450°F. Then reduce heat to 350°F and give them another 10 minutes of baking time. The popovers should be brown and crusty on the outside. I suggest you puncture each with a sharp object to let the steam escape.

Serve hot with lots of butter. Maybe four people?

NOTE: I recently saw cast-iron popover pans for sale. Try muffin pans and then go for the cast-iron.

AN OLD-WAY
BREAD

It is difficult to type this recipe while I have in one hand a huge slice of butter-dripping bread made from the recipe. The recipe brought back memories of the family kitchen and I had another go at baking this bread. The Danes back in my family history had a way with crusty bread. Now you can, too.

1 cup boiling water
1 cup milk, on the edge of boiling
1 1/2 cups rolled oats, regular or
  quick
3 tablespoons butter or
  margarine
2 eggs
1 teaspoon salt
1/4 cup dark molasses
2 packages dry yeast
1/2 cup warm water, 110°F
6 cups all-purpose flour
1 egg yolk (add white to eggs
  above)
1 tablespoon water

In a large bowl pour hot water and hot milk over oats. Add butter, eggs (whole with extra white), salt and molasses. Mix well and let stand for 30 minutes.

Add yeast to a small bowl of warm water. Let stand for 5 minutes and add to the oat mixture. Mix well.

Add flour, a small amount at a time, and beat into mixture. Somewhere between 5 1/2 and 6 cups will be enough to form a stiff dough. Use remaining flour to dust a breadboard. Turn dough out onto board and shape into a large lump. Cover and let rest for 15 minutes.

Now knead bread for 10 minutes until it is smooth. Add flour if needed. Grease a large bowl and drop the dough ball into it. Turn once and return to bowl. Cover and set aside for 1 1/2 to 2 hours.

Punch bread down and turn out onto floured board. Divide dough in half. Place the halves, each shaped as a round loaf, in 2 9-inch round cake pans.

Whip egg yolk with 1 tablespoon of water and paint tops of the 2 loaves. Sprinkle some oats on top of glaze.

Bake in a preheated 375°F oven for 45 minutes. Remove from pan and set on a rack to cool. Not too cool, as it's best when warm. With lots of butter, and some thin slices of sweet onion. What was good back then is still fantastic.

NOTE: One time when I was out of molasses I tried dark Karo syrup and a touch of rum flavoring. An interesting variation. I wonder how good whiskey would do? Maybe in the next cookbook. . .

ALASKA BEER ROLLS

What would be more appropriate than to name these rolls for the state that has the highest per capita consumption of beer, and is as well the largest state in the Union. (Texans, note brag!)

The man who gave me this recipe is a beer drinker, so how come he had any left for bread-making, I'll never understand.

1 package dry yeast
1/2 cup warm milk (about 105°F to 115°F)
2 tablespoons white sugar
6 1/2 cups all-purpose flour
1 8-ounce cup of beer (4 ounces left for you — see?)
4 eggs, separated, with 2 yolks reserved (see NOTE)
1 tablespoon salt
1 4-ounce cube of butter or margarine, softened

In a large mixing bowl dissolve yeast in milk and stir in 1 table-spoon sugar, 2 cups flour and the beer. Cover and let stand over-night.

Beat 2 egg yolks and 2 cups flour into the bowl. Add remaining tablespoon sugar and softened butter cube. Beat egg whites until they are stiff but not dry. Add whites and 2 more cups of flour. Mix well.

Turn out on a lightly floured surface and knead, adding flour as needed, until the dough is smooth and elastic. Grease bowl with butter. Drop the round ball of dough in the bowl and turn once. Cover with moist towel and set in a warm place to double in size, about 2 hours.

Punch down dough. Divide in half. Roll each half into a single long roll. Cut roll into 10 even pieces. Round them and set on a greased baking sheet, about 3 inches apart. Do the same with the second roll of dough. Let stand until the dough doubles again, about 30 minutes.

Slide rolls into a preheated 375°F oven. Bake until they are nicely browned, about 20 minutes. Cool slightly on a wire rack and serve. With beer, naturally.

NOTE: My dog Jake loves to eat leftover fresh egg yolks — they make his coat glossy and he enjoys the royal treatment!

ROADHOUSE BREAKFAST BREAD

Back in the good old days, about halfway between the stagecoach and the gas guzzler phases of personal transportation, Alaska had many prospering roadhouses. They provided beds and good food every twenty or thirty miles along the roads, and even some trails. Folks could spend the night and fortify themselves with a big breakfast for the next day's travel. This type of bread, baked fresh during the night or early morning, gave the clients a good start.

1 1/2 cups warm water
1/4 cup white sugar
2 packages dry yeast
    (2 tablespoons)
1/2 cup warm milk
3 tablespoons butter
2 tablespoons molasses
1 teaspoon salt
6 cups all-purpose flour
1 cup oats, regular or quick
vegetable oil

I start this recipe in the bowl of my powerful mixer. (My arm gets tired.) To the bowl add warm water and 1 teaspoon sugar. Sprinkle yeast on top. Let it stand for 10 minutes.

Add warm milk, remaining sugar, butter, molasses, salt and 2 cups flour. Beat until smooth and then add 3 1/2 cups of flour and 1 cup oats. Continue beating and add just enough more flour to make a soft dough.

Turn dough out on a floured board and knead by hand for 10 minutes. More flour may be added to create a smooth, elastic dough and prevent sticking. Form a ball, cover with a cloth, and let rest for 20 minutes.

Divide dough in half. Roll each half into a rectangle about as wide as a bread pan. Place each half of dough, seam side down, in a well-greased bread pan. Oil tops of loaves, cover and refrigerate until morning.

In the morning preheat oven to 375°F. Take loaves from refrigerator and let stand 10 minutes while oven is heating. If you spot any bubbles in the dough, prick them with a toothpick.

Bake in oven for 30 to 40 minutes. The loaves should be nicely browned and sound hollow when thumped. Remove bread from pans and let cook for 10 minutes before serving. It makes breakfast worth getting up for. Serve with butter and imagination.

CHAPTER 12

FINAL KAPOW

I know it's an awful thing to say about your mother, but mine was a pusher. She pushed desserts! Surely I can say it better. My mother believed every main meal, and some lunches, picnics and even breakfast, should end with something sweet.

I can remember many a breakfast of sourdough hotcakes complete with syrup. Surely these sweet delights should have satisfied her. But no! She would add a large gob of strawberry jam to my plate. Or maybe blueberry jam or the less exotic, in Alaska, salmonberry jam. Kapow!

In my brown paper bag or the metal lunch box I carried to school, I would find other delights. Of course there would be the sandwich of meat, egg or the ever-present peanut butter. This was the mainstay. The Kapow treat could be cupcakes, cookies or, on a hotcake morning, maybe a cold hotcake wrapped around sugar and cinnamon.

Returning home after school, with the hunger of a growing boy, I was usually able to work something special from her. Just enough to hold starvation at bay until dinner.

With dinner there was usually cake or pie, with bread pudding, rice pudding or plain custard filling in at other times. Looking back today, Mother's Kapow list seems endless.

For special affairs, be it a winter holiday or a summer picnic, Mother would outdo herself with desserts. I suspect then family pride had to be served. We always seemed to have neighbors and friends with us on these occasions.

The summer picnic was seldom just a family affair. We would take a group aboard a fishing boat and go to some isolated beach where the group would explode onto the shore. Alaska had and still has many private hideaway beaches.

We kids would scatter to fish, pick berries, beachcomb or just stand around amusing the opposite sex. There was always a bit of storytelling going on — usually on a one-to-one basis, as young men tried to convince young women that they, the young men, were wonderful. Come to think of it, some used the reverse, convincing the young women they, the young women, were wonderful. I merely listened at this age, but I had good retention and found the early training valuable in later life. Little did I know that storytelling would finally become my avocation.

When Mother lifted her huge, hand-operated dinner bell, it could be heard for miles. Kids of all ages forgot what they were doing and ran for the grub.

I never did manage to get first place in the food line. There was this girl with the longest legs and most graceful body you have ever seen. She seemed to float ten feet on every step, or leap. I remember Mother saying, "She will be a great ballerina." To which my father usually added, "Not unless she stops being first in every grub line."

No, there is no love story here. She did learn to control her appetite. She stayed slim and became a great dancer. One of those so graceful and light on their feet you love to hold them in your arms while dancing. Those long legs!

Let's get back to the picnic. A table consisting of three sawhorses and two hatch covers from the ship was loaded with food. Some found decisions difficult. Not me! In fact, at this time I was known as "the bottomless pit"! It was possible to taste everything first, and then settle down to serious eating. The transition from foods to desserts followed the same pattern. If I had to struggle with the last quarter of pie (they served pies in quarters back then), it was still Kapow!

At last came the day when I looked in the mirror and decided I was a man. It was time to break free and go live by myself. I entered a somewhat brief period of my life that I've always thought of as batching. I lived alone in a small log cabin, two blocks off what is now Anchorage's main street, Fourth Avenue. We're talking 1942.

Perhaps you'd be interested in the fittings of this small historical rental unit. I suddenly feel quite old!

The cabin had one door in front, secured by a hasp and padlock when I wasn't home. I suspect everyone in town had a key. I know a lot of girls did. The simple locking system was a great joy to the devilish and simpleminded. Great delight to those who loved to catch you inside and snap the padlock closed. It trapped me successfully, but not always alone. For the first week I was constantly being rescued. In the end I threw the padlock away.

As you stepped through the front door, there was a small wood-burning stove to the right. Along the right wall were a short counter, sink and cupboards. A single faucet gave evidence you had cold city water piped in. On the left side of the cabin were a four-nail coat rack, a table for two and two chairs. Oh yes, a double bed filled up the rest of the cabin. That's all there was room for in the twelve-by-sixteen rental unit.

In case you think I missed a bathroom, you're right. The facility was out back in a small, upright building. Slippers and a path, as the saying went.

It was in this cabin that I first started cooking without someone looking over my shoulder. I mean it both actually and figuratively. The small stove was just large enough for one large pot or two tiny pots. I had a large Dutch oven at the time. I'm sure the cracked lid was all that saved me from a huge steam explosion a time or two.

I also had this old cast-iron frying pan. The numbers on the bottom indicated it was cast sometime in the 1800s. It was worn both outside and inside, but was a cook's delight for the results it turned out. I had to buy only a couple of bread pans and a cookie sheet small enough to go into the tiny oven. I rated it a four-cookie model. I could now create Kapows!

I was scheduled to do a lot of entertaining during my few short months in the cabin. It was equipped for two and when I had guests I suggested, "Bring your own apple boxes!" Yes, they used to be made of wood and they were quite useful after you had eaten the apples.

My batching came to an abrupt end when the U.S. Army found it could no longer do without my services. I was sworn into the Army at 0900 one morning and shipped overseas within the next hour. If this gives you the impression I was flown immediately to be airdropped on Japan, you're wrong. I was sent in a six-by-six truck across Ship Creek to Fort Richardson. To the Army, a thirty-foot-wide creek was a sea.

I wasn't especially thrilled by Army life, but I found the Army and my mother had one thing in common. For the evening meals they served some sort of dessert, a Kapow? Well, maybe a kapow.

My first meal, for those of you who were never served a meal in a mess kit in a field chow line, was instructive. Let me explain. This is the military mind's idea of buffet-style eating. You take what you get!

You approach a line of men armed like yourself, mess kit in one hand, canteen cup in the other. This keeps both hands occupied and you unable to defend yourself. You also don't have to handle the food.

At the first station a larger-than-you-ever-wanted gob of partially mashed potatoes is dumped into the mess kit. At the next station a full ladle of gravy is added, usually missing the potatoes, a feat developed by expert training of serving personnel. The meat is next and could be any one of a number of useful meats. My first meal was pork luncheon meat, although in later meals we would find bacon, ham, pork, mutton, goat and, on occasion, beef. All were allowed to slither down into the gravy.

Another step along the line and you arrived at today's vegetables. It might be peas, corn, green beans or mashed squash. The amount of the serving raised the tide level of the gravy.

I completely forgot the bread, one of the better things in the chow line if you could manage to keep it out of the gravy. Come to think of it, in the gravy might be best. You sure couldn't spread butter on it. Again the military had developed tropical butter: it wouldn't melt. They naturally shipped it to Alaska.

Now comes the Kapow station. On my first meal it was freestone peach halves.

That's one half in a ladle full of peach juice, poured gently over the entire meal. I almost said mess, in the mess kit. It did thin down the gravy somewhat. Bon appétit?

It is my theory, completely unsupported by documentation, that sweet-and-sour sauce was first discovered by a mess sergeant. He served sauerkraut and pineapple the same day. He won more compliments for the meal than ever before in his life. He never served it again, and slept with the recipe under his pillow until the war ended. You can now buy his sweet-and-sour sauce in any market.

One of the high points of my life was the day I passed out of the gates of Fort Richardson, again a civilian. The Army had given me 15 cents, travel pay to get home. The bus ride cost 35 cents, and I was glad to make up the difference.

By now my folks were back living in Anchorage so I went first to their home. Mother had a strawberry shortcake awaiting my return. She still made the best KAPOW!

LONGWAY STRAWBERRY SHORTCAKE

Way back in my youth, before I discovered Bisquick, I actually made strawberry shortcake like this. I would say it was better back then, but people are discovering that taking the time to scratch-build shortcake is both fun and tasty. When I find an interested person, I usually give him or her this recipe. Now, with it in this book, I can make the obvious suggestion, "Go buy my book!" Hey! You already know I wasn't born yesterday.

Making the Cake

2 1/2 cups all-purpose flour
2 teaspoons white sugar
2 teaspoons baking powder
12 tablespoons butter or
       margarine, cut in small
       pieces
2 eggs
1 cup sour cream
1 teaspoon vanilla

In a large bowl sift together flour, sugar and baking powder. Add butter pieces and work in with clean hands until the mixture is blended. Form a well in the mixture and add eggs, sour cream and vanilla. Continue to mix the dough by hand. Turn out onto a floured board and knead for at least 5 minutes.

Roll the dough in a circle about 1/2-inch thick. With a 3-inch biscuit cutter, cut out rounds and place on an ungreased cookie sheet. Keep rolling and cutting until all the dough has been used. Aim for 12 to 14 rounds.

Bake in a preheated 450°F oven for 15 minutes, until nicely browned.

The Topping

4 pints strawberries
2 tablespoons lemon juice, preferably fresh
1/2 cup white sugar
2 cups cream, whipped, or nondairy topping

Pick over the berries and save as many perfect berries as you think you'll need for garnish. At least one for each biscuit.

Mash the remaining berries slightly in a bowl. Add lemon juice and sugar. Mix well and chill.

Building the Shortcake

If you are using real whipping cream, I suggest using a pastry bag with a star attachment. Otherwise, use a spoon to be creative with the topping.

To build an individual shortcake, split a biscuit/cake. Place half on a serving dish and ring its outer edges with whipped-cream topping. Fill the center with strawberry mixture. Place the second half of cake on top and again ring it with topping. Cover it with strawberry mix and top with a mound of cream. Add a whole berry or two on top and serve. Depending entirely on how generous I am with the filling and whipped cream, they will serve six to seven.

NOTE: I've tried, at the dough stage, forming one single large cake. This can then be covered with goodies and cut in slices. It's faster but not so classy.

NELSON FAMILY TOLL HOUSE COOKIES

I would imagine every family in the United States has its own recipe for Toll House cookies, but just in case you don't, here's ours. The major change was the arrival of peanut butter chips in the grocery store. We enjoy the two kinds of chips together.

2 1/4 cups all-purpose flour
1 teaspoon salt
1 cup butter or margarine, room
    temperature
2 eggs
3/4 cup white sugar
3/4 cup brown sugar
1 teaspoon baking soda
1 teaspoon warm water
1 teaspoon vanilla
1 cup chopped nuts, pecans if
    possible
6 ounces semisweet chocolate
    chips (or chocolate mint)
6 ounces peanut butter chips

Sift flour and salt into a large bowl.

In another large bowl combine butter, eggs and sugar. Mix until smooth and well-blended.

Dissolve soda in warm water and add to the mixture. Now mix in flour, vanilla, nuts and chips.

Chill in the refrigerator for at least 1 hour, but longer is okay.

Preheat oven to 375°F. Grease cookie sheets. Drop teaspoonfuls of dough onto the cookie sheets. Keep far enough apart so they will not join when baking, about 2 inches.

Bake each batch about 10 minutes or until golden brown. Keep baking until you run out of dough. Makes about fifty cookies.

NOTE: For even more variety, leave out peanut butter chips and put in more chocolate. Or leave out all chips and increase the amount of nuts. Or try substituting the new chocolate chunks instead of all the chips. For the calorie watchers, try reducing the butter content to half a cup, or even to a quarter of a cup. Either makes an edible cookie. Or try substituting wheat bran for the nuts or chips as well as reducing the butter, and make a health-food cookie. Have fun!

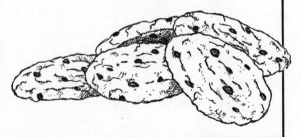

CHINESE CHOCOLATE PEANUT BUTTER COOKIE

I have to admit a certain chocolate and peanut butter candy bar was the inspiration for this cookie. I had this attack, a "non-Mac" type, one afternoon when the car was not running. I had to make something quick. This is it!

1 4-ounce cube butter or
    margarine
4 ounces (1/2 cup) semisweet
    chocolate chips
2 ounces (1/4 cup) peanut butter
    chips
1 tablespoon light corn syrup
1/4 teaspoon vanilla
1 3-ounce can chow mein noodles
3/4 cup chopped nuts, pecans or
    your choice
15 nut halves

In a medium-sized saucepan melt butter. Add chocolate chips, peanut butter chips, corn syrup and vanilla. Stir until everything is warm but the chips are not completely melted.

In a large bowl crumble chow mein noodles. Mix in chopped nuts. Pour warm mixture over noodles and nuts. Stir until well-combined.

Drop large spoonfuls of mixture on waxed paper over a cookie sheet. Press a nut half into each cookie. Slide cookie sheet into refrigerator to firm the cookies. Serve cold, except when under attack. Then it's permissible to try a couple semi-warm.

ULTIMATE KAPOW
(Cheesecake)

I recently met a senior citizen who has found the key to all his neighbors' homes. When he arrives at the door carrying one of his cheesecakes, he is always greeted with open arms. He is invited to every party within three blocks of his home. This recipe might be used in the same manner.

The Pastry

3/4 cup all-purpose flour
1/3 cup butter (key ingredient)
*   or margarine*
2 tablespoons white sugar
1/8 teaspoon salt

In a bowl combine all the ingredients and blend. Press mixture into a 10-inch springform pan. Bake in a preheated 475°F oven for 5 minutes.

The Filling

2 pounds ricotta cheese,
*   well-drained*
1 cup white sugar
4 eggs
1/3 cup all-purpose flour
1/3 cup cocoa
3 teaspoons light rum
1 teaspoon vanilla

Combine cheese and sugar in mixer bowl. Mix at high speed until smooth and creamy. Add eggs, flour and cocoa while continuing to beat. Add rum and vanilla and mix well.

Pour the filling mixture into the pastry-lined pan. Bake in a preheated 450°F oven for 10 minutes. DO NOT open the oven door! Reduce the heat to 300°F and bake another 55 minutes. Turn off the heat but still DO NOT open the oven door. Allow the cheesecake to remain in the oven for another 30 minutes.

Now you can take the cake from the oven, cool it on a rack, and refrigerate until serving time. Serves eight to ten. Serve with real whipped cream and you truly have the ultimate dessert. Real KAPOW!

MABEL'S PINEAPPLE DESSERT

Mabel was a friend of Mother's who always made it a point to spoil me rotten on our visits to her home. I was pleased to find this recipe in Mother's cookbook. I have converted it to modern ingredients so you can join in the Kapow.

4 tablespoons butter
1/4 cup brown sugar
1 can pineapple slices
1 jar small maraschino cherries
1 package buttermilk biscuits
    (4 1/2-ounce refrigerated or
    your own biscuit recipe)
1 8-ounce tub topping, dairy or
    nondairy

Start with individual 10-ounce glass baking dishes. Into each dish add 1 teaspoon butter, 1 teaspoon brown sugar and a slice of pineapple. Add a cherry in the pineapple slice hole.

Divide the biscuit dough. Flatten each section by half, and cover the pineapple slices.

Bake in a preheated 350°F oven for 10 to 15 minutes, until the biscuits are nicely browned. Remove from oven and let each cool for 10 minutes. Invert each dish onto a serving platter. Be generous with the topping and serve. Serves four or more.

MARY JANE'S COOKIE

Mary Jane is a name from my far-distant past. It's but a memory, one firmly planted in my mind, as many such memories are, by food. In this case, cookies. She escaped me but the recipe didn't.

1 4-ounce cube butter or
    margarine, softened
1 egg yolk
1/2 cup white sugar
1 teaspoon almond extract
1 cup all-purpose flour
1/2 cup chopped pecans
pecan halves, one for each cookie

In a bowl combine butter, egg yolk, sugar and almond extract. Beat until light and fluffy. Add flour and chopped nuts. Mix well. Chill for 30 minutes.

Roll dough, a teaspoonful at a time, into 1-inch balls. Place them on a greased and floured cookie sheet about 1 inch apart. Lightly press a pecan into top of each ball.

Bake in a preheated 300°F oven for 25 minutes or until nicely browned. Remove and cool on a rack. Makes 25 to 30 cookies.

BUD'S
BEER CAKE

Bud is the name of my recipe-donating friend. It is not a commercial, unless you want it to be one. Experimentation has proved that any good beer will make a satisfactory cake, a statement open for reconsideration if the price is right. The only real use of the suspected brand of beer was to loosen Bud's resistance to giving me the recipe. I'll rewrite this entire recipe for the right offer.

2 teaspoons baking soda
3 cups all-purpose flour
1 teaspoon ground cinnamon
1/2 teaspoon ground cloves
1/2 teaspoon ground allspice
2 cups dates, pitted and finely
    chopped
1 cup chopped nuts, pecans or
    walnuts
2 4-ounce cubes butter or
    margarine, softened
2 cups dark brown sugar
2 eggs
2 cups beer, preferably flat

In a rather large bowl combine baking soda and all but 1 tablespoon of flour. Add cinnamon, cloves and allspice. Mix well and set bowl aside.

In a second bowl combine 1 tablespoon flour, dates and nuts. Stir to coat the dates and nuts with flour.

In still a third bowl combine butter and sugar. Cream together and add the eggs one at a time. Beat mixture and then add it to the flour bowl with 1 cup of beer, stir well and add second cup of beer. Stir in the nuts and dates.

Pour well-mixed batter into a well-greased and floured tube cake pan. Bake in a preheated 350°F oven for 1 hour and 15 minutes. Test with a toothpick. If it comes out clean, the cake is done.

Remove from the pan and cool on a rack. When completely cool it's edible, but it's better wrapped in foil and rested for 24 hours before serving. Serve with lots of butter and your brand of beer.

NOTE: See the beer drinker's handbook for simple instructions for making beer flat. Or open a can today to make the cake tomorrow. Hide can from everyone else and forget where you hid it for at least 10 hours. This plan has been partially successful, providing there are plenty of unopened cans available in the refrigerator.

COOK INLET
MUD CAKE

At the headwaters of Knik Arm in Alaska's Cook Inlet are the remains of the town of Knik. Yep! People still live there and are proud of it. In the far-distant past this was actually a seaport. But the Matanuska and Knik rivers poured mud into the arm in unbelievable amounts. The man from Knik who named this recipe was surely thinking about how the mud nearly killed a town.

2 cups all-purpose flour
1 teaspoon baking powder
salt
1 1/2 cups strong cold coffee
1/2 cup whiskey, preferably
    bourbon
2 4-ounce cubes butter or
    margarine
5 ounces unsweetened chocolate
1 3/4 cups white sugar
2 eggs, beaten
1 teaspoon vanilla
cocoa

Sift flour, baking powder and a pinch of salt into a large bowl.

In a double boiler over simmering water combine coffee and whiskey. Bring to just short of a boil. Add butter and chocolate and stir until the mixture is smooth. Remove from heat

and stir in sugar. Allow to cool for 5 minutes and transfer the mixture to a mixer bowl. At medium speed add half a cup of flour at a time, blending until well-mixed. Add eggs and vanilla and beat again.

Grease a 9-inch tube baking pan and dust it with cocoa. Pour batter into pan. Bake in a 300°F oven for 1 hour and 30 minutes. Test with a toothpick for doneness. Bake longer if necessary.

Allow to cool in the pan before removing. Serve slightly warm or cold. Have a good dairy or non-dairy topping available as a finishing touch.

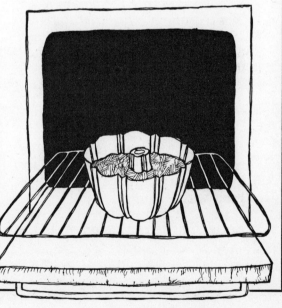

NON-NEWTON
FIG COOKIES

Again my memories of youth come back to me. Back when Fig Newtons were cheap enough to feed to your kids. They were the one treat Mother used to buy instead of make in her kitchen. But as the dollars shrank and the cookie prices climbed, she came up with this substitute recipe. I remember eating her cookies, but when I came across her recipe I found my taste had changed over the years. Sorry Mom! I've made some changes.

2 tablespoons vegetable oil
1 4-ounce cube butter, or
  margarine if you must
1/4 cup brown sugar
1 teaspoon grated lemon rind
1 cup graham cracker crumbs
1/4 cup orange juice
1 tablespoon grated orange rind
1/4 cup strained honey
1 cup finely chopped dried figs
1/2 cup finely chopped nuts,
  your choice

Begin by setting out 20 paper muffin cup liners. With a pastry brush, coat the inside of each paper liner with oil.

In a medium bowl combine butter, sugar and lemon rind. Beat with mixer until creamy. Stir in cracker crumbs.

Distribute this crumb mixture equally among the oiled cups, covering the bottom and as far up the sides as possible. You are making a crust. Refrigerate for 1 hour to firm.

In a saucepan over medium heat combine orange juice, orange rind, honey and figs. Bring to a boil and stir constantly until the liquid thickens.

Start with a teaspoonful of filling in each pastry-filled cup the first time around. Keep going around until the filling is used up.

Sprinkle nuts over the filling and place in refrigerator to cool and firm.

Serve right in the paper cups. Each lucky person can peel his own delight.

NOTE: One day I was out of figs and tried pitted dates, finely chopped. Fantastic. Next I'm going to try pitted prunes, and make a dual-purpose cookie.

CHAPTER 13

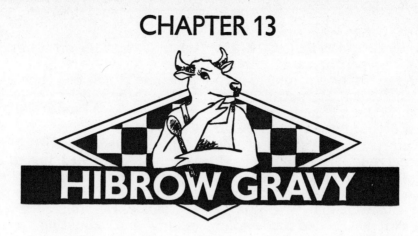

HIBROW GRAVY

Well, what else would you call a sauce you pour over other food? Whether you do it to hide the food or enhance its taste is not important. A fancy sauce is pretty highbrow, but it's gravy.

In fact, I was quite far along in life before I ever heard of *sauce* as something poured over food. It was something that some men drank too much of. In our house we had gravy, at least a dozen forms, which added delight to meats, potatoes, biscuits and anything else that sounded (or looked) better under gravy. Biscuits and gravy, commonly referred to as *soppy*, were one of my favorites.

Mother, always hospitable, often said, "A couple of extras for dinner are no problem. I'll just make more biscuits and gravy." It was like adding a quart of water to the soup; it extended the available food. I especially liked the more-biscuits-and-gravy dinners. The "wadding," as Mother called it, was both filling and delicious.

Mother had a standby she called milk gravy, a favorite of mine, but she never jotted down the recipe. Connie's mother was the only other woman I ever knew who could come anywhere near matching Mom's milk gravy. We neglected to get her recipe, too. I'm sure it isn't lost for all time. I just don't have it.

All of which brings to mind the efforts of a less famous cook, Clarence Rebald, known as "Grits" to friend and foe. He was from somewhere in the Deep South, where it seems people actually like grits. I've been told they prefer grits to potatoes, though I find that impossible to believe.

Grits was a cook, one of the breed who managed to feed the men in the mining camps and the fishing fleet. He was cooking in the Bellyview Mine in south-central Alaska when he came into my life, or I entered his, by stopping to bum a meal at the camp. My patrol duties with the Alaska State Troopers met with the approval of the mine owners, though they seemed to make some of the employees nervous.

At my first meal in Grits's mess tent, I was introduced to black-eyed peas. They were close enough to beans to make a hit with me. He had tried earlier to serve grits to the crew, and caused a near riot. They had him astraddle a piece of railroad iron and were literally riding him out of camp on a rail, when the brave superintendent brought the charade to an end. But the crew had made their point. Black-eyed peas were Grits's compromise, accepted by the majority. The minority reserved comment, but hung over Grits like a flock of vultures waiting for him to die.

Some months later I stopped by the camp again and was lucky enough to hit a biscuit-and-gravy night. Grits and I became friends that evening. I was nearly in tears with the memory of Mom, and he liked people who became emotional about his cooking.

My last visit with Grits was on the night he served Red Eye Gravy over pork chops, which made an instant hit with the entire crew. His battle to bring southern cooking to the Alaska Bush was proceeding well.

On my next visit Grits was gone. Pat Murphy told me the story of his departure. To Grits, the ultimate in southern cooking was whiskey sauce instead of gravy. He had managed to smuggle three fifths of whiskey into this dry camp. On the morning of this eventful day he was up early, working on his masterpiece. I never did get his recipe, although I did get some clues. Step one was to open and taste the whiskey, so he could build the sauce to set off the whiskey taste to its fullest.

Once satisfied with the quality and taste, he combined ingredients, beat, whipped, sampled and cooked the various things required for a superior whiskey sauce. He suffered through much tasting and adjusting, as the sauce seemed hesitant to come to its full potential. Creating the sauce proved to be an all-day process.

At last dinnertime came. The second cook, Al Petri, had prepared the remainder of the meal. The helpers carried it to the table. Al went back to tell Grits it was sauce-serving time, and found him collapsed, face-down in a huge pan of whiskey sauce. Quick-thinking as Al always was, he pulled Grits out of the sauce and began artificial respiration, between breaths instructing a helper to stir the sauce once more and serve it.

Grits was revived and rushed to an Anchorage hospital with serious facial burns, a very high blood-alcohol level and unemployment. I'll always remember Pat's concluding remark, "The sauce was good, but you could hardly taste the whiskey."

Any discussion of sauces must include the saga of Mildred Tollerman. Millie was a large, friendly woman of more than forty years. As she worked in the rougher cafes, she was known tomany more men than women. She always fed well, and many of her customers were heavier than the medical books said they should be. Millie liked well-rounded men.

Sven Iverson was her ideal, six-feet-four and near three hundred pounds, one of those who can never find belts long enough to go around them. (A few of you out there know what we larger men go through.) Still, Sven was a happy man who got along with everyone. Who would spoil a good thing by telling Sven he ought to lose weight?

Millie and Sven found themselves working in the same mining camp, just east of McGrath, in the summer of 1938. Millie was of course cooking. Sven was wrestling a hydraulic monitor, washing gravel into sluice boxes. Gold was the mine owner's objective, but not Millie's. She aimed to make Sven her fifth husband. She made no secret of her intent. Sven always got the choicest steak, the largest slice of pie, the biggest piece of cake. You get the picture.

Sven's objective was limited to making enough money during the summer to see him through the winter. He was aware of his standing with the cook, but he had no intention of getting hooked. He did bring himself to smile at her often and give her a compliment or two, though only so his favored treatment would continue.

The men were about evenly divided. After all, Sven was a square-head and therefore stubborn, but Millie had a track record that included four husbands already. Then came the midsummer evening when Sven got a huge bowl of ice cream drowned in chocolate sauce for dessert. The betting odds changed drastically that night. Most of the men had Sven with a ring in his nose.

The first shipment of strawberries came into camp in late June. Shortcake time was to be Millie's big-gun attack. Millie didn't forget the others; every man in the mess got all the strawberry short-cake he could eat, but Sven made out like a bandit: a dinner-plate-sized piece of shortcake, six cups of strawberries, and a massive serving of real whipped cream!

The men at the table watched Sven shovel the first huge bite into his mouth and smile — with a full mouth, a neat trick in itself. Then his eyes rolled up so you could see nothing but white. Then from somewhere within him came sounds of deep emotion.

The mess tent emptied as the men went off to try to get some new odds on their bets, or at least get more money on Millie than they had on Sven. All but Slippery Sam. He was still taking bets on Sven, and getting odds now. He wandered back to the mess tent just in time to see Millie standing before Sven, holding out a dishwater-clean hand. Al's confidence was shattered when he heard Sven ask, "Will you marry me?"

Acceptance was instantaneous. Within minutes the entire camp was sure Millie had won, although no one was paying off until the wedding bells had rung.

Late that same evening Sam, Sven's tent-partner, found him suffering terrible stomach cramps. They persisted until morning, so an emergency aircraft evacuation was ordered. Sam volunteered to go with Sven. What more could a tent-mate do?

All we know for sure is that Sven vanished the day he was released from the hospital. He was traced as far as Seward, where he boarded an Alaska

Steam vessel headed for Seattle. It seems someone (and only circumstantial evidence points to Sam) had mentioned casually to Sam that Millie's four late husbands had all died of stomach cramps. I'm sure Millie wasn't to blame; it was the fault of poor storage facilities. But I didn't blame Sven for running like heck. After all, discretion is the better part of valor.

Oh yes, Sam was soon back in camp, collecting handsomely on Millie's failure.

SEWARD SEAFOOD SAUCE

In almost every place they serve sauces with seafood, the sauce is cold. This isn't bad, but here's one you can serve hot, and it's well worth a try.

1/4 cup tomato-based chili sauce
1/4 cup lemon juice
1/4 cup butter
2 tablespoons Worcestershire
    sauce
2 tablespoons white sugar

Combine all ingredients in a small saucepan. Bring to a boil over high heat while stirring. Serve at once, hot! The recipe yields about 3/4 cup of sauce. Serves four people.

MILLIE'S WARM MUSTARD SAUCE

Here's the only one of Millie's sauce recipes I ever managed to acquire. Millie always said, "This is not a hot sauce!" She was right, it's served hot but it's not hot like Tabasco. It's a nice mild sauce, excellent on many meats.

1 cup light cream
2 tablespoons dry mustard
1 teaspoon all-purpose flour
1 egg yolk
1 teaspoon white sugar
1/2 cup cider vinegar

In a small bowl combine 1/4 cup cream, dry mustard and flour.

Place a heavy-bottomed pan over low heat and add the remaining 3/4 cup cream. Heat slowly and add the mustard-flour mixture.

Beat egg yolk in a small bowl and dip two tablespoons of cream mixture into the bowl. Mix well and pour the egg mixture into the main pan.

While stirring constantly, add sugar and cook until mixture thickens. Heat vinegar in another pan and add to the mustard mixture. Taste and add salt if you feel it is needed.

Pour into a serving boat and take hot to the table.

NOTE: It can be poured hot over a meat before serving. Or try it instead of a cream sauce over Chicken Scallopini.

MICROWAVE CREAM SAUCE

I owe the creation of this sauce to the microwave oven. It has rejuvenated my interest in discovering new recipes and converting old ones. This is one of the most useful sauces I've ever found and very easy to make. Experiment with it and don't name it after me.

6 tablespoons butter or
    margarine
1/3 cup all-purpose flour
1 teaspoon salt
1/4 teaspoon white pepper
1/4 teaspoon ground nutmeg
3 cups milk
3 egg yolks

In a 2-quart covered glass microwaving dish, melt butter on high setting for 1 minute and 30 seconds. Remove from oven and whisk flour into butter until you have a smooth mixture. Slip into microwave oven again on high for 1 minute.

Remove from oven and lift cover. Whisk in salt, pepper, nutmeg and milk. When smooth, slip back into the microwave on high for 30 seconds. Remove, stir and return every 30 seconds until the sauce thickens. About 5 minutes, but can happen sooner depending upon your oven.

Beat egg yolks in a small bowl and add 1/2 cup of thickened sauce to eggs. Mix well and return bowl contents to the thickened mixture. Microwave at 1/4 power another 5 minutes, stirring several times. Remove and serve whenever you need a white sauce.

NOTE: Add a can of clams and serve over spaghetti or noodles.

For a cheese sauce, add the cheese of your choice as the last step before serving.

Much as I hate to suggest it, you could add a jar of dried beef to the cream sauce and serve over toast. It recreates a dish all you older servicemen will recognize.

MICROWAVE MEAT SAUCE

How I ever cooked for fifty years without the microwave, I'll never understand. With it I can often put a meal on the table in one-third the time it would have taken before. For a busy writer, it's wonderful. I'm not so sure it's great for a fellow who writes cookbooks. Only time will tell. Here's a simple recipe that allows you to turn out a fast, easy meal.

2 tablespoons vegetable oil
2 cups chopped onions
2 pounds ground beef, pork,
  lamb or chicken
1 can Italian stewed tomatoes
1 tablespoon tomato paste
2 teaspoons dried parsley
1 teaspoon salt
1/2 teaspoon black pepper
1/2 cup wine, red or white
1/2 cup tomato sauce

In a rather large glass microwaving dish with a cover, combine oil and onions. Process in microwave for 2 minutes on high. Add meat and continue cooking, stirring every minute for 5 minutes. Add tomatoes, tomato paste, parsley, salt, pepper and wine. Cook another 2 minutes. Add the tomato sauce and return to oven. Stir every 3 minutes until the sauce thickens, usually 12 to 15 minutes.

Remove and serve over rice, noodles, squiggly macaroni or anything else your imagination can discover.

NOTE: It requires very little imagination to turn this into a spaghetti sauce. Add mushrooms, chili powder, oregano, basil, a touch of cumin and you got it.

ORIENTAL FISH SAUCE

I may have mentioned my friend Gene and his constant search for the world's best fish sauce. This is another of his efforts. It has a slight Oriental taste, but he had no idea which culture of the Orient it might derive from.

3 tablespoons minced green
    onions, with some green
8 tablespoons butter or
    margarine, room temperature
1/4 cup dry white wine
1 tablespoon ground ginger
1/4 teaspoon garlic powder
1/4 teaspoon ground coriander
2 teaspoons soy sauce

In a small pan over medium heat, sauté onions in 1 tablespoon butter until limp.

Remove from heat and add remaining butter. When all is softened, add to a bowl containing the other ingredients. Mix well with a wire whisk. The mixture should be creamy and well-blended.

Serve with any fish or seafood dish.

NOTE: It even goes well with canned seafood and the refrigerated leftovers make a great bread spread.

RUSSIAN MUSTARD SAUCE

Most people realize we bought Alaska from Russia years ago. So our history here is full of names, places and ideas the Russians brought, and their descendants keep alive in the State of Alaska today. Many customs and cooking ideas are still in use. Here is an interesting example.

1 ounce dry mustard
1/2 cup white sugar
1/2 teaspoon salt
2 tablespoons boiling water
3 tablespoons strained honey
1 tablespoon cider vinegar
2 tablespoons apple butter

In a small bowl combine mustard, sugar and salt. Add 2 tablespoons boiling water and stir until sugar is dissolved. Add honey, vinegar and apple butter and mix well.

Cover and refrigerate. I usually store it in a small jar as it keeps nicely for three to four weeks.

Use the mustard sauce wherever you've used mustard in the past. It's excellent on ham, but holds its own on hot dogs, beef and even in some salads. Eggs love it.

MEDITERRANEAN WINE-TOMATO SAUCE

There is a neighbor woman down the street who gets excited when they play "Zorba the Greek" on the radio. She passed this recipe on to me. She called it a cooking sauce, and suggested simmering meatballs or hamburger patties in it. She was right and I cooked several different meats in it, including hot dogs. It does more for ground meats, though.

2 1/2 cups water
3/4 cup red wine
1 6-ounce can tomato paste
1 1/2 teaspoons salt
1 teaspoon cumin

Combine all ingredients in Dutch oven. Whip until you have a smooth paste.

Add meat to be simmered. Cook to your degree of doneness and serve with a gravy boat of the sauce on the side.

PETERSBURG TARTAR SAUCE

Way back in my youth, when I lived in Petersburg, it was known as the Halibut Capital of the World. It was a natural to have a tartar sauce named after it. So when this recipe came my way, I remembered.

1/2 cup mayonnaise
1/2 cup sour cream
1/4 cup minced green onions
1/4 cup finely chopped dill
    pickles
1 tablespoon drained and
    mashed capers

Combine all ingredients in a small bowl. Mix well. Cover and chill until used. Can be thinned with a little milk if it seems thick for your taste. Serves four nicely.

Try it on any fish, crab or other seafood.

GENE'S WHITE WINE SAUCE

I'm afraid Gene is going to be difficult, as I've put only two of his fish-sauce recipes in this book. I tell him he should write a cookbook, but he says I've stolen most of his really good recipes. I plead "Not Guilty!" and offer this recipe.

2 cups fish stock
2 cups dry white wine
1 small mild onion, minced
2 cups heavy cream
1/2 teaspoon lemon juice
2 egg yolks, beaten
salt and pepper

In a saucepan bring fish stock, wine and onion to a boil and reduce liquid to 1 cup. Add heavy cream and return to a reduced heat. Stirring carefully, reduce liquid to 1 cup. Add lemon juice and remove from heat.

Cool slightly and spoon several tablespoons of warm sauce into beaten egg yolks. Mix well and return everything to the sauce. Cook again until sauce is thickened. Salt and pepper to taste. Serve with fish.

NOTE: Try this fish sauce with Nelson Quick Fish Poach on page 47.

UMBRAGEOUS STEAK SAUCE

This is definitely an uncommonly good steak sauce. The person who provided the recipe warned me that it is somewhat difficult because it has a tendency to stain stainless steel, erode plastic and ruin any spoon used to stir it. I have found that, while it is not the universal solvent fiction writers dream about, it may be man's best effort in that direction to date.

20 ounces soy sauce
10 ounces Worcestershire sauce
10 ounces Heinz 57 sauce
16 ounces brown sugar
2 teaspoons garlic powder
2 teaspoons onion powder
1 teaspoon black pepper
2 teaspoons lemon juice
1/2 cup prepared mustard
2 teaspoons hot sauce (Tabasco
or your choice)

Combine ingredients in a large glass bowl. Pour into 2 quart jars. Cover one with plastic and a rubber band. Keep the other out for today's steaks.

For a steak you plan on broiling, pour sauce on a plate and dip one side of the steak in the sauce. Broil sauced side. Now lift the steak with a fork and dip into sauce on the raw side. Return to grill, grilled side down. Finish broiling.

It can be used as well for a steak you intend to fry, or brush a little on a pot roast before you brown the sides.

Or when cooking with one of the nylon roasting bags, dip meat in sauce before placing in bag. Add 1/2 cup of extra sauce to the bag, seal and puncture twice. These instructions will cover cooking a chicken or a pair of whole fryers in such a bag.

I even know one man who claims he puts a daub of this sauce behind each ear before going out on a date. I can't claim to have tried this myself.

SO-YOU-LIKE-GARLIC SAUCE

Yes, I do! In fact, I have a couple of recipes that use garlic to the extreme. This isn't one of them, but you do have to like the stuff to even consider trying it. I've found it different with fish. Quite a change.

3 egg yolks
2 tablespoons lemon juice
5 tablespoons white wine vinegar
5 large garlic cloves, crushed
1/2 teaspoon salt
1 cup salad oil (olive is nice)
3/4 cup finely chopped blanched
    almonds

Combine egg yolks, lemon juice, vinegar, garlic and salt in a blender. Blend at high speed for 30 seconds. Add 2 tablespoons oil and blend until creamy. Add remaining oil in a steady stream while blending at high speed.

When it is thick, smooth and creamy, transfer to a small bowl and stir in nuts.

Chill and serve with fish. Should you wish to thin the sauce, use only lemon juice. Try it on vegetables, too.

MARY'S YOGURT-MINT SAUCE

Our friend Mary served this sauce to Connie and me when the meal was based on a pork roast. You can imagine me like a bloodhound after the recipe. I had to promise to make her famous before she'd part with it. So come on, let's make Mary famous.

1 cup plain yogurt
2 tablespoons finely chopped
    fresh parsley (or 1 teaspoon
    dry parsley, crumbled)
2 teaspoons finely chopped fresh
    mint (or 1 teaspoon dry mint,
    crumbled)
1 garlic clove, minced
salt and pepper

Combine all ingredients in a small bowl about an hour before you plan to serve. It makes about a cupful of sauce.

Try on many types of meat, but it's especially good on pork or lamb.

ALASKA BUSH CHOCOLATE SAUCE

People living in the larger communities can drop in to a grocery store for a can of chocolate sauce any time. Not so out there in the wilds of Bush land, or Outback, if you've been Downunder. These people have to create some ordinary delights from scratch, if they have any of this condiment. I remember a few years as a Trooper stationed at an outpost. We shopped monthly and had to plan ahead for at least that far.

Here's a sauce that filled in many times to satisfy hungry-for-something-different kids. It went over cakes, ice cream when available, and snocream like Mother used to make.

1 1/2 cups white sugar
1 can evaporated milk
4 ounces unsweetened chocolate
1 teaspoon vanilla
1 pinch salt

Blending of the ingredients requires a double boiler or a small saucepan in a larger pan of hot, but not simmering, water.

Add all ingredients to the small or top pan and mix until the chocolate and sugar melt. When well-blended, serve hot.

NOTE: To reheat the mixture, add a few drops of hot water and reheat.

CHAPTER 14

HOW NOW

Do you realize that during this year alone, thousands of young people will reach adulthood and be thrust into the world totally unable to cook? They will almost certainly be dependent upon either fast foods or TV dinners! Doesn't it get you right here? A touch lower, please, over the stomach. Your hand was high enough to suggest either being in love or suffering heartburn, two other dangers our youths face during this period in their lives.

I remember the day I cut the apron strings and moved out into the cruel world. I was better off than most youths of my time. I could cook. As this was way back before TV dinners, and even before the Big Mac, you can see how lucky I really was to escape the trauma of starvation in the midst of plenty.

I had learned to cook at home, and practiced aboard the ships the men in my family manned during my early youth. I graduated from cook's helper on the larger ships to chief cook aboard the smaller vessels. Neither my father nor my brother ever progressed past the canned soup and peanut butter sandwich stage of food preparation.

Yes, cooking on an old Shipmate stove in a heavy sea was a challenge that prepared me for cooking on a small stove in a rented cabin. You know Anchorage's four-lane Fourth Avenue of today? My first home-of-my-own was in the second block south, a log cabin on an alley.

During my short occupancy of the cabin I took only one roommate. I was seduced by his declaration, "I like to wash dishes." I didn't like that part of cooking. Next day the dishes didn't get washed and we argued. He went out into the world and he must have got lost. I worried for a while and then forgot. I went on cooking for myself and friends of both genders.

It wasn't long before one of the feminine gender volunteered to cook for me. She brought all the makings down from her house, just up the alley. Oh, you thought . . . This was years ago, you know.

Anyway, she whipped up a great hotcake batter and poured a nice-sized hotcake on the flat spot on the stove. I watched over her shoulder. The hotcake raised and a huge bubble formed and burst, but she still hadn't turned the hotcake. Soon smoke filled the room. Cooking lesson: do not kiss the neck of the cook who's baking hotcakes. It is a gross waste of food and it can delay a meal almost indefinitely.

It was either open the cabin door or die of smoke inhalation. As we stepped outside to breathe, one of my male friends arrived. His timing was awful. I pretended I was glad to see him, and even invited him into the smoke-filled cabin. He stayed a week. She stayed only long enough to pack her stuff and depart, never to return.

My male guest couldn't cook, and this led me to a conclusion. There's a mothers' conspiracy. They teach their daughters to cook, right? So these daughters go out into the world with a skill that attracts men. I know there are some women who go out with an even more powerful attraction, beauty! And some women have both beauty and cooking skill. We men are really defenseless against a well-armed woman.

So the male who can't cook is an easy target for the first young (or even not-so-young) woman who comes along. She can often lead him to the altar by the nose — a nose where the smell of both her perfume and her cooking is entrenched forever. I've been best man at a number of those weddings. I knew I was the best man, because I could cook.

You want an example? I'll give you my buddy, Carl. His total cooking experience was frying two eggs. They started as over-easy and came out scrambled, mainly because he had trouble with the toaster. It was one of those in which you toast the bread on one side, then lower the side of the toaster and the bread slides down, so when you close the toaster the bread gets toasted on the other side. Why am I explaining a toaster you can now find only in a museum? Carl ate the eggs anyway.

Carl had a short attention span in the kitchen, but great concentration in the pursuit of women. He went to the wall with a proposal right after a well-cooked and well-served dinner. She looked up at him through soft eyes and said, "Yes!" I was best man one more time.

The U.S. Army was willing to do the cooking for me, and for those millions of young men who couldn't cook for themselves. The Army knows about my theory. You might think that, with my meals cooked and served, I would have more time to chase women. Wrong! The first thing the Army did was remove me from the general flow of civilization for eight weeks. During the ninth week I discovered that a woman can forget a man completely in eight weeks. My first five telephone calls brought "Gordy who?" It was ego-deflating. I had been reduced to just another GI with ideas.

Then I discovered some women who had never learned to cook at their mothers' apron strings, and they were fascinated with a man who could cook. I could respect a woman who turned out her daughter to fight on even terms with males, and I was soon to have one of those women as a mother-in-law. Dancing was what brought Connie and me together. I proposed; we were married when she got old enough. I went to work; she stayed home and learned to cook. As children joined us, Connie found herself working full-time as a mother, and she taught our daughters to cook.

My traveling as a State Trooper kept me out of the kitchen most of the time. Now that I've retired, Connie has gone out to work in the real world. I do most of the cooking, so she can be a lady of leisure after she comes home. You know, from the living room, "Let me know when dinner's ready, Honey." As I've mentioned once or twice before, turnabout is fair play. Don't you agree, ladies?

This arrangement gives me days free to write, experiment, and try the recipes that now seem to flow in like water after the dam bursts.

So it is to all you non-cooking people out there that this chapter is dedicated. The recipes are simple as possible and utilize such modern shortcuts as canned and packaged foods. Try these and branch out when you feel comfortable in the kitchen. Enjoy!

SPAMBALAYA
(Jambalaya)

This is a recipe I put together one night long ago, when I had a limited meat supply. I've had occasion to make it many times, but I must admit, seldom exactly the same. It lends itself to changes. It's always tasty.

2 tablespoons butter or
    margarine (or vegetable oil)
2 cups chopped celery
1 cup chopped onions
2 garlic cloves, minced
2 1/2 cups water
1 teaspoon salt
1/2 teaspoon dry, crumbled
    parsley
1/4 teaspoon crumbled or ground
    thyme
1 bay leaf
1 can stewed tomatoes, Italian or
    regular
pepper
1 cup uncooked rice
1 can pork luncheon meat (Spam)

Start with a large frying pan or even better, a Dutch oven. Over medium heat melt butter and sauté celery, onions and garlic. When the onions are tender, add water, salt, parsley, thyme, bay leaf, tomatoes and pepper. Stir carefully, add rice and stir again.

Cover and cook over low heat for 30 minutes.

Dice Spam into 1/2-inch cubes and add to pan. Continue cooking another 10 to 15 minutes, until rice is done.

Remove from heat, take out bay leaf and serve. Will serve four to six people.

NOTE: Substitute ham for Spam, or make the meat a cup of sliced salami strips. And if you're like me, add a can of mushrooms to the dish.

EASY SCALLOPINI
(Chicken)

I used to create scallopini with a great deal of fussing and attention to detail. I had a special sauce I thought was a necessity. But no longer, as this recipe is so simple and it's easy for anyone to produce a good dish. Try it!

3 tablespoons bread crumbs
    (seasoned packages okay
    but ...)
2 tablespoons grated Parmesan
    cheese
salt and pepper
vegetable shortening spray
4 chicken breast halves, skinless
    and boneless
1/2 cup white wine (sherry okay)
1 can cream of chicken soup

On a piece of wax paper combine bread crumbs and grated cheese. Season to taste with salt and pepper. (If you use seasoned bread crumbs, disregard the salt and pepper.)

Spray the bottom of a nonstick frying pan with vegetable shortening. Place pan over medium heat. Press both sides of each chicken breast in bread crumbs and cheese to coat well. Place in pan to make a single layer.

Cook about 4 minutes on one side until a golden brown. Turn and brown the other side for 3 minutes. Remove chicken to a serving platter and keep warm.

Pour wine into frying pan and bring liquid to a boil. Reduce to about half the original volume. Add chicken soup, right from the can. Stir well and heat until just hot. Pour sauce over the chicken breasts and serve.

I think it's a two-person dish, but I imagine it could be stretched to four. You could serve biscuits to soak up the extra sauce. Soppy!

QUICK CHICKEN GUMBO

The company shows up unexpectedly and you find they came for dinner with full confidence that you could work miracles in the kitchen. With such a degree of confidence, they are probably good friends. If not, throw them out. If yes, reach into the cupboard for those emergency supplies and whip this one out.

3 cups cooked rice (instant okay)
1 15-ounce can Italian stewed
*   tomatoes*
1 8-ounce can tomato sauce
1/4 teaspoon hot sauce
*   (Tabasco)*
1 bay leaf
1/2 teaspoon thyme
1/2 teaspoon salt
1 package frozen okra, cut in
*   pieces*
3 5-ounce cans chunky-style
*   chicken*

Start by preparing the rice and set aside to finish cooking. Follow package instructions.

In a medium-size saucepan over medium heat combine tomatoes, tomato sauce, hot sauce, bay leaf, thyme and salt. Bring to a boil and add okra. Cover and just simmer for 10 minutes.

Add chicken chunks with juice and cook another 5 minutes to blend flavors.

Serve over freshly cooked rice. Serves four easily.

NOTE: Out of okra? Use chopped frozen broccoli. I've even used shredded cabbage and had raves from the eaters. Experiment!

TURKEY CHILI

Recently I ran across a package of ground turkey meat in the supermarket. I had to try it. This was the result.

vegetable shortening spray
1 1/2 pounds ground turkey (or other meat)
1 cup chopped onions
2 garlic cloves, minced
1/2 teaspoon crumbled oregano
1/4 teaspoon black pepper
1 1/2 tablespoons mild chili powder (hot if you must)
1/2 teaspoon salt
1 6-ounce can tomato paste
1 15-ounce can Italian stewed tomatoes, drained (save juice)

Lightly spray a large nonstick frying pan and place over medium heat. Add meat and break up into small pieces as it browns. When it is free of any red coloration, drain the excess fat.

Stir in onions, garlic, oregano, pepper, chili powder, salt, tomato paste and tomatoes.

Bring to a boil and cover. Reduce heat and simmer for 15 minutes. If it's too thick, thin with some of the tomato juice. If too wet, cook a bit longer to reduce liquid content.

Serve in bowls with slices of good bread. Serves four.

NOTE: If you were to add a can of red beans during the last 5 minutes of cooking, it would serve up to six.

CASSEROLE DELIGHT

Everyone who cooks should have at least one casserole recipe that can be used in any emergency. This was my old standby recipe, somewhat reduced in size from the years when we were feeding a minimum of eight.

8 ounces noodles, medium-wide
4 chicken thighs
1 can cream of mushroom soup
1 can cream of chicken soup
1 cup milk
salt and pepper

You will require a 3-quart casserole dish or a covered glass bowl.

Place uncooked noodles in the bottom. Lay chicken thighs on top of the noodles.

Combine the 2 cans of soup and cup of milk. Season to your taste. Pour the mixture over chicken and noodles. Salt and pepper to taste. Cover and bake in a 350°F oven for 60 minutes. Remove, check noodles for doneness. Extra time up to 20 minutes might be needed. When noodles are done, return to oven for 10 minutes uncovered to brown the top.

Take casserole dish to the table. Serves two.

MUSHROOM CREAMED CABBAGE

I realize cabbage isn't the favorite food of many people, usually for the wrong reasons. Yet this simple recipe has changed many a mind on the subject of cabbage.

1 cup water
2 tablespoons butter
1/2 teaspoon salt
1/2 head cabbage, about 2
*   pounds, cut into 4 pieces*
1 can cream of mushroom soup
1 4-ounce can mushrooms,
*   drained*
pepper

In a covered skillet over medium heat, combine water, butter, salt and cabbage. Bring to a boil and boil partially covered for 5 minutes. The water should be almost gone and the cabbage tender but not soggy.

Add mushroom soup and mushrooms and stir into the cabbage. Cook for another 5 minutes until hot. Dish up in 4 bowls. Make pepper available. Serves four.

APPLE/HAM/ SWEET POTATO NONPIE

This recipe came to me in the mail about a year ago. I didn't get around to trying it until recently. I can't imagine why I waited so long.

1 16-ounce can boneless ham,
*   cut into 8 slices*
2 tablespoons vegetable oil
1 17-ounce can sweet potatoes,
*   drained and sliced*
2 16-ounce cans pie apples
2 tablespoons brown sugar

In a skillet over medium heat, brown ham slices in oil. Leave in the skillet and arrange sweet potato slices over ham slices. Spoon apple slices over sweet potatoes. Sprinkle brown sugar over the apples.

Cover skillet and cook over low heat until the contents are heated through, about 10 minutes.

Remove from heat and take the skillet right to the table. Serves four of the hungriest people you've ever fed. Taking the pan lid off is like ringing a dinner bell.

RED FLANNEL HASH
(Corned beef hash)

So many years ago I hate to count them, the cook aboard a cannery tender showed me this recipe. He considered it a Sunday dinner special. I surprised growing kids with it from time to time. It usually got a mixed reception until they tasted it. Comments were different the second time around.

1/4 cup cream (or evaporated
    milk as aboard ship)
1/8 teaspoon black pepper
1 16-ounce can diced beets
1 pound potatoes, boiled and
    cubed 1/4 inch
1 12-ounce can corned beef,
    diced 1/4 inch
3 tablespoons vegetable oil (or
    bacon grease as aboard
    ship)
1 cup chopped onions
1 garlic clove, minced

In a large bowl combine cream, pepper, beets, potatoes and diced corned beef. Mix lightly.

Add oil to a frying pan over medium heat. Sauté onions and garlic for 5 minutes. Pour potato-meat mixture into the frying pan and smooth to an even layer. Reduce heat and cook contents until hot. Do NOT stir, so the bottom of the dish will brown.

Place a serving plate upside down over hash in the frying pan. Carefully invert hash onto the plate. Serve at once to four to six people.

NOTE: If served for breakfast, fry eggs in another pan and garnish the hash before serving.

BACON
CORN BREAD

Here's a recipe I know to be more than fifty years old. I used it to feed my older brother and Dad aboard the crab fishing ship. It's a quick, filling meal for hungry folks.

1/2 pound bacon, cut in 1/4-inch
    cubes
1 1/4 cups cornmeal
3/4 cup all-purpose flour
1 tablespoon baking powder
1 tablespoon white sugar
1/2 teaspoon salt
1 egg
1 cup milk (or 1/2 cup evapo-
    rated milk and 1/2 cup
    water, as used aboard our
    ship)

Drop diced bacon into a cast-iron frying pan and slide into a preheated 400°F oven. Cook until bacon pieces are crisp. Drain bacon and reserve grease.

In a large bowl combine cornmeal, flour, baking powder, sugar and salt. Carefully stir in egg and milk. Do not overwork the dough. Add 2 tablespoons bacon grease and the bacon bits to the dough. Fold them in easily. Pour mixture back into the frying pan.

Return pan to the oven and bake 20 minutes, until the top is golden brown. It should be springy to the touch. Remove from oven, cut in wedges and serve right in the pan. Serves up to four people.

NOTE: Make lots of butter available, as well as strawberry jam, or even maple syrup for some.

OLD COUNTRY BEEF AND NOODLES

The original recipe was designed to feed four people with very little meat. The noodles provided the major nourishment. I converted to more meat for modern tastes.

3/4 pound noodles, medium-
    wide
1 pound lean ground beef
1 cup chopped onions
2 garlic cloves, minced
1 8-ounce can tomato sauce
2 teaspoons prepared mustard
8 ounces sour cream

Begin by cooking noodles as the package directs. With luck they should be done about the time the remainder of the dish is ready.

In a large frying pan over medium heat, cook meat, breaking it into pieces as it browns. Stir in onions and garlic and cook another 5 minutes until tender.

Add tomato sauce and mustard, stir and cover. Cook for another 5 minutes at a simmer.

Remove from heat and gently stir in sour cream. Drain noodles and spread on a platter. Pour the meat sauce over noodles and serve. Serves four.

CHAPTER 15

WHISTLE WETTERS

Way back when I was a youth, the act of consuming alcohol was known as wetting your whistle. That saying may still be viable in some places. My kids and grandkids at least know what it means, but they look upon me as one of the ancient mariners when I use it. I didn't treat *my* father that way! True, I find some of the kids' useful terms mystifying, but I fight back by suggesting they are quaffing their beer.

You have to watch the women nowadays. They call on quite a vocabulary in emergencies, and what is more, they can spell the words they use. Still, the appearance of Trivial Pursuit® has helped me convince one and all that I'm almost as smart as my wife, Connie.

With a few notable exceptions, our family has never been known for its heavy drinking. We're social drinkers. If a neighbor accidentally produces an

exceptional batch of beer, he can always count on us to help him celebrate. I can remember one, maybe two, success celebrations.

Yes, I learned early to use alcohol wisely. Well, there was one slip in my training effort. About the time I went to batching, I made the mistake of letting someone else fill my glass. He was already drunk, and he let the whiskey pour long after the mixer bottle went empty. With my taste buds already deadened, I didn't detect the straight whiskey until too late. I knew I was in trouble.

Naturally there was a woman in this story. She was sitting on my left, and suddenly her face went all out of shape. Later they told me I was rude enough to say, "You've had too much to drink. Your face is getting all fuzzy!"

I woke up in my bed, alone and

hurting. My head was at least a foot wide, and someone had stuffed an old sock into my mouth. I looked in the mirror. No, it wasn't a sock, it was just my tongue. At this point my whiskey-pouring friend showed up to take care of me, and he had the audacity to admit having poured my drink the night before. I indicated by words and feeble gestures that as soon as I recovered, he was in deep trouble. Even so, he taught me a valuable lesson: pour your own!

I followed that rule for many years, with two exceptions. The first was the night I made staff sergeant in the Army. The scene was the NCO Club (Noncommissioned Officers); the booze was three-point-two beer, and we all thought it was impossible to drink enough of that to get drunk. You could buy only opened bottles of the stuff, and you couldn't take them from the club. When the bar closed there were thirty-six open bottles of beer on the table, and as the guest of honor I did my part to face the challenge.

I have no memory of getting to the barracks that night. They told me later that I led the group in song all the way, and we were shushed by two MPs. At the barracks I had

insisted, as platoon sergeant, upon tucking each of my men into bed. I had no memory of that, either, and it scared the heck out of me. A guy in such a condition could kill and not know it! The one saving grace was that everyone said I was a happy drunk, not a fighting drunk, but it didn't take a lost weekend to make a near-teetotaler out of me.

The second exception was another promotion party, when I made staff sergeant again, this time in the Troopers. I had learned to trust my wife to pour me a drink when I was busy discussing policy with the other Troopers, and I thought she had filled the glass that suddenly appeared at my elbow. Wrong! Another drunk had poured me a drink, and again the mixer bottle had gone dry! This time I caught it, and Connie drove me home. I didn't sing on the way, Connie tucked me into bed, and I swore never again.

I still enjoy making a drink or two once in a while. In fact, I was into winemaking when a couple of my cookbooks were written. Even yet we usually pick lowbush cranberries in the fall and make a fantastic liqueur.

As I was growing up I heard the men speak of whiskey as a survival fluid, a sort of antifreeze for the body. In this land of near-total darkness through long hours of the winter days, we have two temperatures to consider. One is what the mercury thermometer reads on the sheltered side of the house. The other is the chill factor, calculated by using the still temperature and the strength of the wind blowing across the land.

For instance, at ten above it's cold, but add a twenty-knot wind and the chill factor is twenty-five below zero. Get down into the below-zero temperatures, say minus twenty-five, and add wind, say that same twenty knots, and your chill factor goes way down to seventy-five below. You need more than a shot of alcohol to keep you warm.

In fact, alcohol makes the low temperature more dangerous. Every winter we have a few drunks who lie down in the snow and sleep their way into eternity. The only time alcohol can help is after a long spell out in the cold, when you come in to stay for the night. Hey! A hot buttered rum can really hit the spot.

There *are* drinks that can actually help in cold weather. While I was stationed in Glennallen with the Territorial Police, I ran into my first sixty-below weather. Just keeping the patrol car running at that temperature is a full-time job. You never, but never, let it cool. I was fortunate enough to have a garage which, with a heater going full blast, we could hold at forty degrees inside. The stove oil of the day would get too thick to flow at times, and even adding kerosene as a thinner didn't always work.

One morning I opened the garage door and found it forty below inside.

The heater had gone out. Fortunately the car engine hadn't cooled as fast as the air. It started. While it was warming up I went back into the house. Connie had my emergency supplies ready, including a quart thermos of coffee. I poured a cup of coffee from the pot, considered adding a shot of rum, and decided I didn't need a handicap on such a cold day.

Two hours later, some forty miles up the Richardson Highway, I found a couple sitting in a cold car. They were lightly dressed and had a single thin blanket they'd wrapped themselves in. The inside of their car had come down to the outside temperature, which the thermometer taped on my antenna base said was sixty-seven below.

Sitting in the front seat of the patrol car with me, with the heater going full blast, they started to get warm. I reached into the back seat and recovered the thermos of coffee. Had it been the most expensive liquor in the world, it wouldn't have held a candle to the coffee I poured for this thoroughly chilled couple. So you see, "whistle wetters" come in many forms, and not all are alcoholic.

Over my two winters patrolling out of Glennallen I made a lot of friends with my thermos of coffee. I was concerned for the thirst of my fellow man then and while I was writing my other books, and the concern continues.

OUR HOUSE CREAM LIQUEURS

When a number of Connie's friends and Connie became interested in the appearance of new cream liqueurs which suddenly were being promoted, I took one look at the price and shuddered. It was into my files and out with a recipe, one I had never tried, but it looked promising. I whipped out a few samples. They were successful and, while expensive, nowhere near the asking price in the local booze stores.

Whiskey Cream Liqueur

1 3/4 cups whiskey (Irish, Scotch, rye or Bourbon. Okay! Try rum or brandy)
1 14-ounce can sweetened condensed milk
4 eggs
2 tablespoons chocolate-flavored syrup
2 teaspoons instant coffee crystals
1 teaspoon vanilla
1/2 teaspoon almond extract

Place all ingredients in a blender and mix until well-blended and smooth. Serve right from the blender over ice. Refrigerate any leftovers (Ha!). Use inside of one week.

Liqueur Cream Liqueur

1 3/4 cups liqueur (mint, coffee, orange or almond)
1 14-ounce can sweetened condensed milk
1 cup whipping cream
4 eggs

As above, place all ingredients in a blender and mix until smooth. Serve and keep as above.

CORDIALS
TO COMFORT
THE HEART

A Christmas gift of Strawberry Cordial from a lady without a strawberry bed was a pleasant surprise. It moved me to get the recipe. Two years of near-constant heckling was required to weaken her will. Or she liked to hear me beg. Who says all good things don't come to him who waits! And heckles! I learned the latter skill from Connie.

2 10-ounce packages frozen
    strawberries (or blackberries
    or raspberries), crushed
1 lemon, peel only, scraped clean
    of white membrane and
    sliced
3 whole allspice berries
1 cinnamon stick
1 cup brandy
2 cups vodka
1 cup sugar
1/2 cup water

In a large glass jar combine crushed berries, lemon peel, all-spice, cinnamon, brandy and vodka. Cover jar and set aside for two weeks. Filter liquid through a coffee filter and return to the jar.

Combine sugar and water and cook into a syrup. Pour syrup into the alcohol mixture. Bottle and let mature for a month. All right, taste a small glass fresh, and then compare the matured product.

LIQUEUR DE TANGERINE

Out of every box of tangerines that comes into our home at Christmas, we pick six big, plump fruits. They are set aside to make this liqueur. The recipe, or a version of it, has drifted down through Connie's family. Or so she tells me, and it's her family so she should know.

3 cups vodka
1 whole clove, lightly crushed
6 tangerines, peeled carefully, with all the white membrane from the peel scraped off. Chop the peel fine. (Eat the fruit. We don't need it!)
1 lemon, peeled and treated like tangerine peel
1 cup white sugar
1/4 cup water
food coloring (yellow and red)

Into a large glass jar with a cover, pour vodka. Add the clove, and tangerine and lemon peels. Set aside for two weeks to a month.

Strain liquid through a coffee filter and discard clove and peels. Cook sugar and water into a syrup, cool and add to vodka liquid. Add a drop of yellow coloring and a drop of red to the liquid.

Bottle and set aside for a minimum of two weeks to mature. Serve sparingly, as your bottle can vanish in even a crowd of six.

CHINATOWN PUNCH

As I am a pineapple lover, this recipe caught my eye when I opened my morning mail. I was off right after breakfast to gather the makings. It was worth it to watch my companions at dinner the night the punch was served.

4 cups unsweetened pineapple juice
4 cups water
1 can pineapple chunks and their juice
1/4 pound fresh ginger, cut in small chunks
3/4 cup white sugar
1/2 cup lemon juice

In your punch bowl combine pineapple juice and 2 cups water. Add juice from the can of pineapple.

In a blender place 2 cups of water and ginger chunks. Purée the mixture and pour through a strainer into punch bowl. Discard strained contents. Add sugar and lemon juice to punch. Set aside to chill for a couple of hours.

At serving time add a couple of pineapple chunks to each glass and fill with punch. It serves eight nicely.

NOTE: If a guest demands alcohol, add a jigger of vodka and rename it Chinatown Piledriver.

MONK CORDIAL

The first word is monk, as in the Benedictine Order. I could tell you this is a recipe handed down from father to father for a thousand years. Who knows, it might even be true.

1 1/2 cups vodka
6 crushed anise seeds
3 tablespoons angelica root
    (Try your health food store.
    Use ginger if you absolutely
    have to.)
1 tablespoon unsalted almonds,
    finely chopped
1 whole allspice berry
1 cinnamon stick
1 teaspoon crushed marjoram
    leaves
1 cup white sugar
1/4 cup water
food coloring (red and yellow)

In a large jar with cover, combine vodka, anise, angelica root, almonds, allspice, cinnamon and marjoram. Set aside for a minimum of one week, but shake or stir daily.

Strain liquid through a coffee filter and return to the jar. Cook sugar and water to make a syrup. Cool and add to the vodka liquid. Add one drop of red and one of yellow food coloring to the liquid.

Seal and set aside for a month to mellow. Serve with pride.

FISHERMAN'S XMAS PUNCH

I have to admit to dipping a cup into a bowl of this punch at a young age. Well, the kid at whose house the party was going on dared me. I think he wanted me to be caught in the act. After one sip I slipped the cup to my older brother and he covered the transaction nicely. He was a dependable older brother.

I hadn't remembered the incident until I ran across this recipe in Mother's cookbook. It's credited to Sara Peterson, at whose house I was sneaky.

3 cups white sugar
1 cup water
1 cup lime juice (bottled lime
    concentrate)
2 fifths dark rum
1 fifth brandy
1 1/2 cups peach-flavored
    brandy
3 fifths champagne (or club soda)

In a large pan over medium heat combine sugar and water. Bring to a boil and cook until it clears. Add lime juice and let syrup cool.

All the other ingredients must be chilled before assembling them into the punch. Pour into punch bowl and add syrup. Have plenty of ice to float in the bowl. Serves twenty.

NOTE: This is a high-alcohol punch and may not be to everyone's liking. Reduce concentration and expand the amount of punch by doubling the amount of mixer or soda. Eliminate the idea of champagne entirely.

COFFEE AND IRISH PUNCH

My mother, and therefore yours truly, is a direct descendant of the 153rd monarch of Ireland. I long have suspected this monarch was king only of that land he could reach with a flight of a well-shot arrow from the topmost tower of his castle, but few who came out of Ireland have anything on me.

True, the blood has been considerably thinned since his granddaughter reached America, but give me a wee bit of Irish whiskey and I can almost speak Gaelic. Have two cups of this and you'll be swearing you can understand me.

12 whole cloves
3 pieces cinnamon stick,
approximately 4 inches in
length each
6 cups water
1/2 cup light brown sugar
1/2 cup coffee, instant or
espresso
1 cup whiskey, Irish (at least for
the first batch)
2 cups cream or half-and-half
1 cup heavy cream, whipped
ground nutmeg

Tie cloves and cinnamon sticks in a cheesecloth bag and place in a large pan over medium heat. Add water, sugar and coffee. Slowly bring to a boil. Reduce heat and simmer for 5 minutes.

Remove pan from heat and take out spice bag. Slowly add whiskey and the half-and-half or cream. Mix and pour into a heat-resistant punchbowl.

Ladle punch into handled mugs, top with whipped cream, and sprinkle with nutmeg.

Serves twelve.

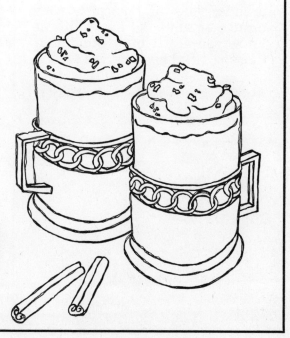

NON-TEQUILA GRANDE

I am one of those people, and I know I'm not alone, who cannot tolerate tequila. It leaves me with a splitting headache after only one drink. I have found I can join the other whistle wetters at a Mexican feed with this drink.

1/4 cup grapefruit juice
1/2 cup orange juice
1 tablespoon lime juice
2 ounces whiskey or vodka
2 teaspoons grenadine
orange slices or sprig of mint

Put the first 5 ingredients into a blender and mix well. Pour into a grande glass and garnish with orange or mint. No one will ever know you aren't busy building a massive headache. Serves one.

BELOW-ZERO JUMP START

Back in my youth when we had few garages, starting the family car in the morning could be a trying experience. All too often breakfast got lost in the shuffle to get the engine started and go to work. This quick, nutritious drink could get the body and mind started as well.

1 cup milk, whole or 2%
1/4 cup smooth peanut butter
1 banana, peeled and cut in
    chunks
2 teaspoons sugar
    (2 teaspoons NutraSweet® if
    you're dieting)
4 ice cubes

Combine milk, peanut butter, banana and sugar in your blender. Mix until smooth. Add ice cubes and blend until ice cubes are crushed. Serve from blender pitcher.
NOTE: Some Sunday morning when you are not going anyplace, try adding a jigger of your favorite alcoholic beverage to the blender.

CHAPTER 16

UNAVOIDABLES

When I was writing each of my other cookbooks, I found myself nearing the end with a pile of recipes that didn't fit into any of the chapters. I classified them as Leftovers and made them into a final chapter.

The same thing was about to happen with this cookbook. When I mentioned it to Connie she grinned and said, "It's unavoidable. You always want to give them more information, whether they want it or not!"

I remember when, back in my childhood, Mother made a similar comment. I came home a winner, but the condition of my body and clothes proved that the other kid had put up a good fight. Mother said, "For you, fighting is unavoidable."

At that point in my life she was right. My father had sat me down and explained many of the things I would encounter in this world, including fighting. He said it was unavoidable if I wished to move through life with self-respect. He did mention that fighting usually results in pain, and that pain discourages fighting, especially if it's administered to the other fellow fast enough. He explained about bullies, those large males who get pleasure from inflicting pain on others. They enjoy fighting because the pain is going one way — to the other guy. Don't be one of those. And when you have to take on a bully, apply the maximum amount of pain in the shortest possible time. Pain is the only deterrent they understand.

I was a bit confused, as I assumed the bully would be working under the same set of rules. After I came home with a knot on my head (a knot of knowledge, Dad called it) the instruction continued:

"When it comes to the point where a

fight is unavoidable, you have to make up your mind to fight. It doesn't matter how big the other fellow is. He may win, but Son, make sure he knows he's been in a fight. Make him pay in pain for whatever he does to you. Make him pay too much for the satisfaction he gets out of winning. If the price is high enough, he'll never want to take you on again, and those people who see the fight will think twice about tackling you."

I discussed this with my older brother. The fourteen years between us had given him time to test Dad's theory. He agreed, and added some of his own: "Don't be belligerent, be friendly, and don't act scared. Try to talk your way out of a fight. Be concerned for the other fellow. Tell him you wouldn't want to hurt him. That does strange things to his confidence; some of it seems to melt and run away, and he'll usually start looking for a way to avoid getting his head pounded. Give him a loophole, a way to get out of it without showing the white feather, and show you're not afraid of him.

"One thing more: if a fight is unavoidable, make your first blow count. One well-delivered, well-placed blow can often end a fight quickly."

I returned to school the next day prepared to fend off bullies right and left. To my surprise, I discovered that sidestepping a fight can be developed into a fine art. Then, too, word of my previous successes had gone before me.

Then came one of those unavoidable challenges. I didn't throw the first punch, because I'd thought I was winning with my mouth. It was there, on my unprotected mouth, that the fist hit me. I got up off the ground, put my head down, and charged into the middle of the red blur in front of me, intent on reaching and smashing the rather large nose that dominated the blur. I felt the jars in my shoulders as three massive blows found their target. They stopped, the red haze lifted, and I found my man sitting on the ground holding both hands over his nose. Blood was oozing through his fingers. I had won the fight!

My reputation was made. No one wanted to take me on for the "fun" of fighting, and I wasn't looking for that kind of fun. That was my last fight in grade school.

We moved to Anchorage then and I had a whole new school to prove myself to, but I was no longer the skinny kid. I was one hundred and seventy pounds of muscle, trained in boxing by Dad and my brother. They tapped for real during practice.

I stepped lightly for two weeks, and then came the unavoidable — an invitation to meet in the alley. I tried the talking tactic. His confidence didn't shake. He threw the first punch. It was poorly delivered, as if he expected to scare me to death with it. My first blow was aimed neatly at his nose, but he stepped back and got it right on the jaw. His eyes rolled up and he crumbled. "My God! I've killed him!" I thought.

Two of his buddies lifted him to his feet and shook him awake. As his eyes regained life he looked at me and, of all things, grinned. "You win!" he said. "You can really hit!"

That was the only fight I had in four years of high school. No one wanted to tangle with me, and I didn't get any fun out of inflicting pain. I was a happy guy, interested in good times and girls.

In a few more years I had the talking technique down to a science. It is a skill I've found useful all my life. I entered my profession, law enforcement, by joining the Alaska Highway Patrol, forerunner of the present State Troopers, and in twenty-one years as a Trooper I never really had a fight. True, I was 230 pounds on a six-foot frame, and I carried a lethal weapon, but my voice and a smile solved many a serious situation without serious difficulty. They provided the loophole for a trapped and frightened individual to slip through and still hold on to a little pride. When the cop is smiling, a man can lay down a weapon without fear of getting shot.

So much for the wild, wild West — or, rather, wild Alaska.

At this point in life I think I know the unavoidable when I see it. There was no way I could avoid writing this chapter without causing myself pain.

So try some of these on your friends, remembering that the firstest with the mostest could be the leastest painful.

SOUTH ANCHORAGE DIP

We were living in South Anchorage when a neighbor brought a chafing dish full of dip to our party. The crowd of people gathered around the chafing dish drew my attention. Armed with a crisp potato chip, I advanced on the dish and managed to scoop up a reasonable amount before the crowd descended again. After one taste I went in search of the recipe like an eagle swooping down on its prey. Would you believe a sea gull after something good to eat? Try it!

1 4-ounce cube butter
1/4 pound provolone cheese,
    very thinly sliced
2 cups canned beans, red or
    kidney, smashed smooth
4 jalapeño peppers, finely
    chopped
1 teaspoon jalapeño pepper juice
1/2 cup minced onions
2 garlic cloves, finely minced

Combine butter, cheese and beans in a chafing dish and heat until mixture is hot. Carefully stir in remaining ingredients. Allow to mellow at least 15 minutes before serving hot to your guests. Serve with tortillas or corn chips. Or it can be used as a topping for other appetizers.

EARLY CALIFORNIA CHOCOLATE

Anyone reading about the early days of California is sure to have seen mentioned the wonderful chocolate served then. I remember Louis L'Amour writing about it in one of his novels. A very few days after I had the book, Connie set a glass of California chocolate down beside me. I tasted it, understood why it was so popular, and wondered is it still common down there?

6 teaspoons unsweetened cocoa
6 tablespoons white sugar
1 dash salt
2 cups hot water
3 cups milk, hot
1 teaspoon vanilla
1 egg, beaten
1 dash nutmeg
1 dash cinnamon

In a pan over low heat combine cocoa, sugar, salt and water. Stir and cook for 3 minutes. DO NOT allow it to boil. Remove from heat.

In a larger pan combine hot milk, vanilla, egg, nutmeg and cinnamon. Mix these together and then pour into the hot cocoa mix. Beat with a wire whip until the mixture is frothy.

Serve at once to two to four people.

NOTE: The last step can be accomplished in a blender if one is available.

GARY'S CASSEROLE TOPPING

For years I fussed over various ways of topping a casserole dish, with minimum, if any, success. Then one day at Gary's house we had a casserole and I liked the topping. He handed me the recipe. Man can do no more for a friend.

2 cups water
2/3 cup yellow cornmeal
2 eggs
3 tablespoons butter or
    margarine
1/4 teaspoon salt
1 1/2 cups grated Cheddar
    cheese

In a bowl mix one cup of cold water and cornmeal. In a pan over medium heat bring the other cup of water to a boil. Gradually add the first cornmeal mixture to boiling water. Stir constantly until it's thick.

Remove from heat and whisk in eggs, butter, salt and cheese. Spoon over the top of your casserole. Bake at 375°F until topping is browned. Use the toothpick test. If it comes out clean, it's done.

GREEN GREEK DIP

In the summers, our gardens are rich in those wonderful greens that will die with the first touch of frost. All too soon, to my way of thinking. This recipe allows some of them to be eaten often and quickly. Besides, it tastes great.

1 bunch spinach, about 6 ounces
    washed and finely chopped
1 bunch Swiss chard, about 6
    ounces washed and finely
    chopped
1 8-ounce carton plain yogurt
1 tablespoon chopped onions
1/4 teaspoon crumbled dill weed

Dry spinach and chard as well as possible. Combine all ingredients in a bowl, mix well and chill for 1 hour.

Serve with whatever other vegetables your garden might supply — cauliflower and broccoli flowerets, carrot sticks, turnips sliced thin and tomato and cucumber slices.

TELEPHONED COLESLAW DRESSING

A few months ago my telephone called me and I answered to hear voices telling me how much they enjoyed my cookbooks. I could have stood there with the receiver pressed to my ear for hours. Instead I was soon copying down a recipe. I asked for permission to share the secret with the world and was authorized to do so. I tried it and found it fantastic. So, World, here it is:

1/2 cup mayonnaise
1 teaspoon white sugar
1/4 cup milk
1/3 cup pickle juice (poured off a
*   jar of sliced cucumber*
*   pickles, without straining)*
Lawry's seasoned salt

Combine mayonnaise, sugar, milk and pickle juice in a bowl and mix well. Add seasoned salt to taste.

Serve over your favorite coleslaw salad makings.

GRANDMA'S SIMPLE SALAD DRESSING

Connie's great-grandmother had this recipe in her cookbook. She was evidently satisfied with a simple recipe that tasted good.

4 tablespoons olive oil
1/2 teaspoon salt
1 dash pepper
2 tablespoons lemon juice (or
*   cider vinegar)*

Pour oil in a bowl and whip in salt and pepper. Add lemon juice and serve over lettuce, shaved cabbage, cold string beans, asparagus or whatever is available.

NOTE: As time went by, she evidently continued to experiment with the dressing. Penciled below was, "Onion juice or Worcestershire sauce." Progressive? I like the thought!

SUMMER SWEET 'n' SOUR DRESSING

In the summer, when the garden is doing well, we sometimes get tired of the same old dressings. Here's one that will regenerate pleasure in eating salads. I open a refrigerator to see a jar of this and my mouth waters. Try it.

1/2 cup vegetable oil
1/3 cup red wine vinegar
2 tablespoons white sugar
1/2 teaspoon salt
1/2 teaspoon celery salt
1/2 teaspoon coarsely ground
     black pepper
1/2 teaspoon dry
     mustard
1/2 teaspoon
     Worcestershire
     sauce
1/4 teaspoon hot sauce
     (Tabasco)
1 garlic clove,
     finely minced

Combine all ingredients in a jar with a screw top. Shake well. Refrigerate. Shake the jar again just before pouring over salad.

ATTENTION-GETTER DIP

While I watched the fellow create this dip I gradually came to the conclusion that he was off his rocker. He kept giving me these superior grins. You know, the kind that can be so irritating. I almost gave up and went home except, being a dedicated food explorer and recipe collector, I had to stay for the ultimate test, the taste.

1 small green pepper
1 large green pepper
4 ounces cream cheese
1/2 cup sour cream
1/2 cup minced onions
1 garlic clove, minced
4 drops hot sauce (Tabasco)
1/4 teaspoon Worcestershire
    sauce
1 tablespoon finely chopped
    chives
salt

In oven under broiler cook smaller green pepper. Turn often until outer skin is burned all around. Remove from oven and drop into a paper bag. Close the bag tightly and allow to cool.

When the cooked pepper is cooled, remove from bag and carefully peel off outer skin.

Cut pepper in half and remove stem, seeds, and interior membranes. Cut the remaining pepper into fine dice.

Combine cream cheese, sour cream, onion, garlic, hot sauce and Worcestershire sauce in a blender. Blend well. Turn out into a small bowl. Stir in the pepper bits and chives. Salt to taste.

Cut the top off large pepper, and remove interior seed and membrane. Fill with mixture and serve.

NO MOTHER
BREAD PUDDING

My mother loved to make bread pudding, mostly because it was a favorite with my father. Or was it the other way around? This is one recipe she never would have imagined. It was served to me aboard a small ship a few years ago, and you know I pinned the cook in a corner and demanded the recipe. The little fellow graciously jotted it down for me.

1 cup minced onions
10 tablespoons butter or
    margarine, room temperature
8 toasted whole wheat bread
    slices
2 cups grated Cheddar cheese
4 eggs
3 1/4 cups whole milk
1/4 teaspoon salt
pepper

In a small pan over medium heat, sauté the onions in 2 tablespoons butter until limp.

Spread remainder of butter on slices of toast. Cut toast in quarters and arrange enough of them on the bottom of a 7-by-11-inch baking pan to cover pan. You should have just one layer of toast.

Sprinkle half of onions over first layer of toast. Add half the cheese to this layer. Repeat the process by adding another layer of toast, onions and cheese.

Combine eggs, milk and salt in a bowl. Add pepper to taste. Mix well and pour over toast layers. Let set for 10 minutes so all the toast soaks up the liquid.

Bake in a preheated 325°F oven for 40 minutes. It should be golden brown and standing tall. Serve hot to four or six. It's good with whipped cream.

OLD ENGLISH YORKSHIRE PUDDING

This is traditionally served with prime rib roast, but can be made and served with any red meat roast, even game meats such as moose, caribou or buffalo. It can make an interesting addition to a festive meal.

2 eggs, room temperature
1 cup all-purpose flour
1 cup whole milk, room
*   temperature*
1 teaspoon salt
meat drippings

Combine eggs, flour, milk and salt in a bowl and beat until smooth and small bubbles form on surface.

Remove meat from roasting pan and turn your oven up to 400°F.

Pour off meat drippings and remove most of the fat. Spoon about 4 tablespoons of the defatted meat drippings into a shallow 7-by-11-inch baking pan. (If drippings are sparse, supplement with melted butter.) Slip pan with drippings into the oven for about 5 minutes to get hot. Remove and pour batter right on top of the drippings. Quickly return baking pan to oven for 30 to 35 minutes. The results should be puffy and golden. Serves eight.

NOTE: To make smaller individual puddings, use a 12-cup muffin pan. Divide the drippings and batter equally into the cups. Bake the same.

AUNT MARTHA'S CORNED BEEF

Aunt Martha was a close friend of Connie's great-grandmother, who crossed the plains on the Oregon Trail back in the covered wagon days. It was quite a trip in those days before trains, cars and airplanes. I, for one, am willing to assume she knew what she was talking about when she passed out a recipe for corned beef. Like a corned bear recipe I've given you before, this one starts out with a hundred pounds of beef.

7 pounds pickling salt
3 pounds sugar
1 ounce saltpeter
1 ounce cayenne pepper
2 ounces baking soda
3 gallons water
100 pounds beef

Combine ingredients, except beef, in a large pot and bring to a boil. Skim off surface until the liquid is clear. Cool to cold.

Cut meat into useable-sized pieces and pack in a keg. Pour the liquid over it. If one recipe isn't enough to cover, make up a second one. Do not thin the liquid with water. All the meat must be covered. Place a plate in the keg to hold meat under the liquid. A large rock on the plate will keep everything submerged.

Meat should cure for 2 to 3 weeks. Remove from liquid only as used.

BROWN BAG PIZZA
(Calzone)

It was a rare occasion during the years our kids were growing up when we didn't have lots of company on pizza days. Leftover pizza was rare, too. When there was a slice left over, usually it was slipped in someone's brown paper school-lunch bag. The lightbulb over my head came on and I sometimes made pizza aimed right at those lunch bags. Like this:

1 cup warm water (110°F)
1 package dry yeast
1/2 teaspoon salt
3 tablespoons vegetable oil
3 1/2 cups all-purpose flour
12 ounces Mozzarella cheese
6 ounces Monterey Jack cheese
1/4 pound ham, pepperoni, fried
    hamburger or any sausage
2 garlic cloves, minced
1/2 cup chopped onions
1/4 teaspoon dry oregano,
    crumbled
1/4 teaspoon dry marjoram,
    crumbled
1/4 teaspoon dry thyme,
    crumbled
1/4 cup chopped or sliced olives
cornmeal

In a heavy mixer with a dough hook, begin the dough. Warm water and yeast are first. Wait 5 minutes before adding salt and 2 tablespoons oil. Turn on the mixer to slow and begin adding up to 3 cups of flour. Mix to a soft dough.

Flour a board and turn dough out onto it. Knead until smooth, adding flour to prevent its becoming sticky. Grease a bowl and turn the dough to coat all sides. Cover with a damp cloth. Set in a warm place to rise to double in size, about 1 hour.

Punch dough down and divide in half. Shape one half into a ball. Roll the dough with a rolling pin into a 12-inch circle.

In a bowl combine cheese, meat, garlic, onions, oregano, marjoram and thyme. Mix well and pour half the mixture over half of the first dough circle. Spread half the olives over the mixture. Fold dough over the mixture side and seal around edges. Roll them to seal completely.

Grease a baking sheet and sprinkle with cornmeal. Add pizza and bake in a preheated 400°F oven for 15 to 20 minues. It should be well-browned.

Do the same with the second half of the dough.

Allow pizza to cool and then refrigerate until lunch-making time. Slice and slip each slice into a sandwich bag, and then into the brown paper bag.

Your kids can drive others wild by having homemade pizza for lunch. Oh, all right, try a slice hot as it comes out of the oven.

ALASKA BROWN SNOWBALLS

These are not snowballs for throwing, so eat them instead. They are different enough to make a hit with your guests.

1 cup grated semisweet chocolate
1 quart vanilla or chocolate ice cream

Spread the grated chocolate on waxed paper.

With freshly washed hands dripping with cold water, form each section of ice cream into a ball and roll it on the chocolate. Place each ball on a cookie tray lined with wax paper. Get the balls made and into the deep-freeze in the shortest possible time. They should firm again rapidly.

At serving time, place each brown snowball in a small bowl and top with more grated chocolate, or chocolate syrup, and whipped cream, nuts or whatever.

Serves eight.

WHITE MONKEY
(Milk Toast)

As you may have guessed, I'm fascinated by old recipes and ways of cooking. Not too long ago Connie received from her cousin a really old cookbook. It had belonged to her grandmother or great-grandmother. No one is quite sure. Many of the recipes are written in ink that is fading rapidly. The script is great, as back then they taught children how to write properly. I'll try to give this to you just as Grandma entered it in her cookbook. The only difference is, I'll do it on a computer so it's easier for us modern people to read and understand. If Grandma could see me, she'd never believe it.

Pour a pint of milk into a double boiler and place over medium heat. As soon as the milk is warm, stir in a teaspoon of flour with two tablespoons of cold water.

As the milk gets hotter add slowly, so as to dissolve it, two ounces of cheese, grated or chipped fine. Then add one tablespoon of butter, a teaspoonful of salt, a dash of cayenne pepper and one egg, well-beaten and mixed with two tablespoons of cold water.

Let the mixture simmer for 5 minutes and then serve hot over brown or wheat bread. The bread should be well-toasted and buttered.

As you see, it's a simple recipe. Your mother may have served you something like this in your youth. Wouldn't it be nice if your kids had memories like ours.

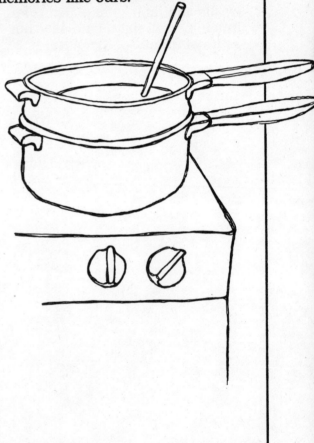

It is Connie's and my hope that this collection of stories and recipes finds favor in your mind. Not all of these recipes are from the past, but we've mixed in some maybe to give you the idea that people have been cooking since "Og" the caveman, and cooking is one of modern man's strongest ties with the past.

With the lightning-fast pace of our world's technology, a hundred years from now none of the cooking techniques from the past may be in use. It is my hope that a few of you out there will keep alive our great cooking history.

Excuse me, the microwave just buzzed to tell me dinner is ready. Enjoy!

INDEX

DID YOU MISS THE MOOSE?

If *HIBROW COW (More Alaskan Stories and Recipes)* gave you the "final kapow" or made you "pie-eyed," *LOWBUSH MOOSE (And Other Alaskan Recipes)* will open your eyes to "beans, beautiful beans" and other culinary delights. *LOWBUSH MOOSE* was the first collection of Nelson's Alaskan recipes and tales.

SMOKEHOUSE BEAR (More Alaskan Recipes and Stories) followed the moose, and you wouldn't want to miss Nelson's zesty Alaskan pasta or the spicy details of his "meatball saga."

And then came *TIRED WOLF (And the Recipes He Pursued)*, Nelson's third cookbook, which is full of "no bull — try beef." Here are just a few recipes: Aleutian Caviar Pancakes, Midnight Sun Shrimp Curry, Chitina Liver Meatballs, and Tomoto's Greek Spaghetti.

Check your local bookstores for Gordon Nelson's humorous recipe collections, or call us toll free at 1-800-331-3510. Write us for a free catalog of our books at the following address:

Alaska Northwest Books™
A division of GTE Discovery Publications, Inc.
P.O. Box 3007, Bothell, WA 98041-3007
(206) 487-6100 • 1-800-331-3510